MW00624262

ADVANCE PRAISE FOR
CHRIST IN EVERY HOUR

"Anthony Sweat is a scriptorian, a storyteller, and a champion for Christ—three characteristics that qualify him in my eyes as a humble expounder on the subject of grace. I loved this book from cover to cover and have found myself contemplating how I might access the power of the Atonement more frequently in my own life. Anthony's ability to show how the Atonement intersects with everyday life left a lasting impression on my heart. Each chapter led me to a deeper understanding of how relying on the Atonement could become a transforming experience. I won't soon forget that Christ isn't only a name; it can become a title that will remind us of the ever-present powers He has to offer us."

—Emily Freeman, bestselling author of *Celebrating a Christ-Centered Easter* and *Becoming His*

"With great insight, Brother Sweat teaches that as simply as we can spell *Christ* we can remember our constant dependence on Him and His constant devotion to us. This is a wonderful book that provides real answers to real questions and will surely make a real difference. The title says it all: We need Him every hour!"

—Brad Wilcox, associate professor of teacher education at Brigham Young University and author of *The Continuous Atonement* and *The Continuous Conversion*

"Anthony Sweat renders a great service in this work, particularly by focusing on how through His grand condescension, our Lord and Master can *identify* with us, identify with our challenges and our crosses, identify with our anxieties and our alienation. As Brother Sweat points out so effectively, because Jesus entered into mortality and opened Himself to all the terrors and temptations that accompany this second estate, He is in a powerful position to succor us, to sooth and settle our troubled hearts, and to save our souls. This book is important. I recommend it highly."

—Robert L. Millet, professor emeritus of ancient scripture at Brigham Young University and author of *Living in the Eleventh Hour* and *Grace Works*

"*Christ in Every Hour* provides unique ways of involving Christ's Atonement in our lives. Anthony Sweat forthrightly supports the doctrine that we cannot separate Christ's Atonement from Christ Himself. This book can make a daily difference in our lives through very thoughtful and creative ways to learn, ponder, and act upon core doctrine and principles related to Jesus Christ's divine influence and power."

—Richard Neitzel Holzapfel, professor of Church history and doctrine at Brigham Young University and coauthor of *Jesus Christ and the World of the New Testament*

CHRIST IN EVERY HOUR

CHRIST IN EVERY HOUR

ANTHONY SWEAT

DESERET
BOOK

Salt Lake City, Utah

Library of Congress Cataloging-in-Publication Data

Names: Sweat, Anthony, author.
Title: Christ in every hour / Anthony Sweat.
Description: Salt Lake City, Utah : Deseret Book, [2016] | ?2016 | Includes bibliographical references and index. | Description based on print version record and CIP data provided by publisher; resource not viewed.
Identifiers: LCCN 2015045489 (print) | LCCN 2015044479 (ebook) | ISBN 9781629734194 (ebook) | ISBN 9781629721996 (hardbound : alk. paper)
Subjects: LCSH: Atonement—The Church of Jesus Christ of Latter-day Saints. | Jesus Christ.
Classification: LCC BX8643.A85 (print) | LCC BX8643.A85 S94 2016 (ebook) | DDC 232—dc23
LC record available at http://lccn.loc.gov/2015045489

Printed in the United States of America
Publishers Printing, Salt Lake City, UT

10   9   8   7   6   5   4   3   2   1

To the memory of President Boyd K. Packer,
a great Apostle, teacher, and artist
who has influenced millions—
and my life's work in particular

CONTENTS

Introduction
THE EVER-PRESENT POWERS OF CHRIST 1

Chapter 1
THE CLEANSING POWER OF CHRIST 7

Chapter 2
THE HEALING POWER OF CHRIST 29

Chapter 3
THE RESTORING POWER OF CHRIST 49

Chapter 4
THE IDENTIFYING POWER OF CHRIST 71

Chapter 5
THE STRENGTHENING POWER OF CHRIST 93

Chapter 6
THE TRANSFORMING POWER OF CHRIST 115

Conclusion
THE AGENT OF CHRIST'S ATONEMENT:
    THE HOLY GHOST 137

ACKNOWLEDGMENTS 154

NOTES 155

INDEX 162

*The Atonement of Christ . . . is an ever-present power
to call upon in everyday life. . . . The Atonement
has practical, personal, everyday value.*

—President Boyd K. Packer

THE EVER-PRESENT POWERS OF CHRIST

I need thee every hour,
Most gracious Lord.
—Annie S. Hawkes

How would you respond to the following question:

Why do I need Jesus . . . today?

In the Church we commonly sing, "I need thee every hour."[1] So why do we need Jesus this very hour, or the next hour? The next day? Unless we are going through a very difficult time in our lives, or entangled in heavy sin, or death is near, for some this "every hour" aspect of the Atonement isn't quite so clear. Yet President Boyd K. Packer taught that Christ's divine influence "is an ever-present power to call upon in everyday life," and that "the Atonement has practical, personal, everyday value."[2]

So what does that look like for us today? Let's talk *reality* here. What ever-present power from Christ can my wife and I receive as we run the day-to-day operations of our home? What infinite power does the Lord offer today to my dear friends dealing with infertility? What ever-present power does the Atonement have for someone with ever-present back pain? Yes, the Lord can and does heal physically, but what does he bring *today* to someone who, despite their faith, isn't physically healed and endures in suffering? What does the Savior do for someone who repeatedly struggles with their imperfections? Related to that, where does the Atonement come into effect not just for the sinner, but also the sinned against, such as the innocent person who has been devastated by a loved one's actions? And let's not overlook another small segment of Saints—what does Jesus do today for those for whom "all is well," those who are currently blessed with a good marriage and children, friends, personal health, comfortable living circumstances, and not involved in major sin? *Overall, what does it look like for the everyday person to need Jesus every day?* These are the questions this book seeks to address.

As I have searched the scriptures and the words of the prophets for answers, I have been drawn to various examples that display Jesus's divine grace in daily operation—multiple stories and teachings where someone was assisted by the powers of Christ. People are raised from the dead and forgiven for mistakes. However, people are also healed in a variety of ways, physically, emotionally, and spiritually. Tears of sorrow are turned to tears of celebration. The hopeless are somehow given hope. Wrongs are made right. Believers are given divine protection and guidance. Needs are met. Comfort is provided. Followers of Christ are given power to do good works they otherwise couldn't have done themselves. Disciples such as Peter and the people of Mosiah have their very natures and dispositions changed. The scriptures seem to teach us that the powers of Christ are many and varied and available for multiple situations and uses in our everyday encounters.

Each chapter of this book discusses one of the Lord's more encompassing divine powers, addressing how the Savior has that power, why we need it in our daily lives, and how we can begin to access that power today. While grace is free (see Romans 5:15–16), we nonetheless must "access by faith into this grace" (Romans 5:2). It is my hope that you will act on the suggestions within each chapter to open up the daily doors of divine influence Jesus is continually knocking on (see Revelation 3:20).

Each chapter on the Lord's powers discussed herein could easily be an entire book in itself. While trying to provide doctrinal depth, I've only used sufficient examples to get the point across, but there is much, much more to glean from in our scriptures and in the words of the prophets. As such, at the end of each chapter I've provided suggestions for further study—scriptures, talks, questions, and invitations to act that can lead to further insight on the subject.

The Savior has something to offer every person, every day, every hour.

It is both my experience and my testimony that the Savior has something to offer every person, every day, every hour. The Atonement of Jesus Christ is gratefully there for all of us who are stained by sin and long to be spotless. But it is also there for those who are hurt, holding out for healing; for those who have faith in a God that is fair but who innocently suffer in a world that often isn't; for those burdened believers who seek strength to meet their daily challenges; for those who think that nobody understands their particular situations but wish that someone would; for those who yearn for personal growth and transformation, for their characters to be more like Christ's; for each of us who, in our unique situations, need Jesus's divine grace and power this very hour—and every coming hour.

THE CLEANSING POWER OF CHRIST

Inner purity is the first and basic element of spirituality. Whether apparent saint or sinner or somewhere in between, each of us has need of and can be blessed today by Christ's comprehensive cleansing power. Perhaps you are struggling under the burden of perfectionism, critically conscious of your many shortcomings and self-condemning because of them. Or maybe you are berating yourself for committing the same sins over and over and wondering whether God will forgive you—again. Conceivably you may be or have been involved in major sin, with the weight of that violation hanging about your neck like a millstone, and you doubt if God will ever fully forgive you. Whatever the situation, the scriptures attest that because of Christ there is no sin that cannot be everlastingly erased, fully forgiven, and completely cleansed. Owing to the Lord's cleansing power, no matter our shortcomings, we can attain and always retain a remission of our sins and be completely clean. That's what he faithfully promises to us, if we faithfully promise to him. Some may wonder if this is possible. The answer is that "with men this is impossible; but with God all things are possible" (Matthew 19:26). Here's how.

Chapter 1

THE CLEANSING POWER OF CHRIST

God pardons like a mother, who kisses away
the repentant tears of her child.
—Henry Ward Beecher

O nce while teaching a class I wanted to help my students understand their everyday, fallen need for Jesus. "We all have sins," I told my class, and beginning with myself I then started pointing to each of them, saying, "You are a sinner, and so are you, and so are you, and you," going up and down the rows. Some students didn't listen, others smiled and laughed, and a few shot back disapproving glares of "How judgmental!" with their eyes. I then came to one of the purest, most Christlike students I have ever taught, and, poking a little fun—because, like biblical Ruth, all knew of her virtue—I said, "Even you, Hillary, are a sinner." The class laughed at the seeming incongruity of my claim. I smiled at my own lame sarcasm. And then Hillary dropped her head and sincerely said, "I know I am. . . . I know." At that moment she taught the rest of us Pharisees in the room a profound lesson:

"And he spake this parable unto certain which trusted in themselves that they were righteous, and despised others: Two men went up into the temple to pray; the one a Pharisee, and the other a publican. The Pharisee stood and prayed thus with himself, God, I thank thee, that I am not as other men are, extortioners, unjust, adulterers, or even as this publican. I fast twice in the week, I give tithes of all that I possess. And the publican, standing afar off, would not lift up so much as his eyes unto heaven, but smote upon his breast, saying, God be merciful to me a sinner. I tell you, this man went down to his house justified rather than the other: for every one that exalteth himself shall be abased; and he that humbleth himself shall be exalted" (Luke 18:9–14).

Being tempted to not closely apply this foundational power of cleansing might say something indicting about ourselves. Those who think they have no sin or don't have a real need to repent may be the ones most in need of cleansing. "If we say that we have no sin, we deceive ourselves, and the truth is not in us" (1 John 1:8). With more than a little sarcasm, Jesus taught a group of murmuring legalist Jews that "joy shall be in heaven over one sinner that repenteth, more than over ninety and nine just persons, which need no repentance" (Luke 15:7). Perhaps some of those who heard him or who have read that verse missed the message, even today: There aren't ninety-nine people who need no repentance. We all do. There are only people who *think* they have no need for repentance. Christian author John MacArthur wrote: "This is the theme of the gospel according to Jesus: He came to call sinners to repentance. . . . Those who think they are good enough—those who do not understand the seriousness of sin—cannot respond to the gospel. . . . The unmistakable message is that Christ's gracious call to salvation is not extended to those who view themselves as righteous."[1] *Only when we become clearly conscious of our everyday weakness do we become clearly conscious of our everyday need for Christ* (see **Ether** 12:27). To become one with Jesus, we must first realize we aren't part of the ninety and nine (*see Study Suggestion 1*).

On the other end of the spectrum, however, there are those of us who think we are so spiritually flawed that we cannot ever stand fully approved before God. We are more than conscious of our abundant sinfulness to the point of utter hopelessness. We think our sins and shortcomings are too serious and/or occur too frequently. The adversary can lead such a person away from Christ with his deceitful whisperings: "God is displeased

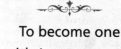

To become one with Jesus, we must first realize we aren't part of the ninety and nine.

with your constant faults. He's frustrated with you. He's given you too many chances and you keep failing. You know better, but look at how weak you are! God's not going to forgive you. Not for that. Not again. You should be better by now. The road back is too far, too long, too hard. If you try, you'll fail anyway. It's time to give up." Those words may be an overexaggeration for some, but for others, sadly, they are not. Those words actually understate the terrible mutterings of the evil one, who tries to crush the souls of all he can. To the disciples who may have lost hope—either because of serious sin or repeated sins, or both—the Lord's comprehensive and continual cleansing power can overshadow those dark thoughts with the light of his love. The scriptures repeatedly attest of our Lord's divine power and disposition to cleanse us freely, frequently, and fully.

There is a great gospel tension here: we must be clearly conscious of our own daily shortcomings and need for repentance, but be completely confident in Christ's divine ability to daily cleanse us of those very weaknesses. Both elements are absolutely critical to availing ourselves of Christ's continual cleansing power and of obtaining a daily hope in his salvation. The purpose of this chapter is for both the apparent saint and sinner (and everyone in between) to understand our daily need for the cleansing power of Christ and how to attain and continually retain that holy power. To do so we must first understand something fundamental about our dear Lord's divine cleansing character.

Christ *Freely* Forgives Our Sins

From the moment Jesus was born, his ministry was centered on his unique spiritual cleansing power. Jesus's very name says as much. To Christ's earthly father, Joseph, an angel told him: "Thou shalt call his name JESUS: for he shall save his people from their sins" (Matthew 1:21). The very first recorded word Jesus ever preached in public was "repent" (Matthew 4:17). The Lord lovingly reminds all of us in our weakness and sin, "My bowels are filled with compassion towards [you]" (D&C 101:9). Micah informs us that the Lord "delighteth in mercy" (Micah 7:18) or, as Elder Jeffrey R. Holland of the Quorum of the Twelve Apostles has said, "The thing God enjoys most about being God is the thrill of being merciful."[2]

As such, Jesus "frankly forgave" all who sincerely sought forgiveness (Luke 7:42). Clearly repentance was (and is) required, but upon a commitment to forsake sin, Christ forgives liberally, generously, and without restraint. This is one reason why Jesus attracted the spiritual outcasts of society: publicans, women of questionable morality, thieves, zealots, and the like (see Luke 15:1). Although Jesus's followers and disciples were a catalog of commandment breakers, there was something inviting in the Lord's nature that made them want to be near him. A cleansing power emanated from him that caused the spiritually impure who longed for purity to be drawn to him.

As I read the Lord's modern scriptural voice in the Doctrine and Covenants, I often find myself surprised how repeatedly and quickly—even unexpectedly—the Lord grants forgiveness. Regardless of the revelatory topic, the Savior often inserts a merciful "thy sins are forgiven." A revelation on the last days and millennium? It begins with "your sins are forgiven you" (D&C 29:3). The elders want to know which way to travel on a journey? "Your sins are forgiven you" (D&C 60:7). Establishing the First Presidency? "Their sins are forgiven them" (D&C 90:6). It is estimated that "on more than 20 occasions in the Doctrine and Covenants, the Lord told those to whom He was speaking, 'Thy sins are forgiven thee,' or similar words."[3] Talk about a freely forgiving nature!

Christ *Frequently* Forgives Our Sins

When Jesus detects a contrite and repentant heart, the Lord's cleansing power is not just given *freely*, it is also given *frequently*. Jesus's answer to Peter about how often we should forgive people was actually an insight into the Lord's own character: I am confident we could accurately rephrase the question as, "Lord, how oft shall we sin against you, and you will forgive us? till seven times?"

and Jesus would reply, "I say not unto thee, Until seven times: but, Until seventy times seven" (Matthew 18:22; see also v. 21), suggesting limitless forgiveness. That is great news to all of us who struggle with repeated sin. Perhaps no better scriptural record exists of the Lord's frequently forgiving nature than those related to Joseph Smith. Surprising as it may seem to some, the Lord repeatedly forgave the Prophet of the Restoration—for matters both large and small. The Prophet was conscious of his personal shortcomings, as was the Lord, who lovingly said of his young servant, "In weakness have I blessed him" (D&C 35:17). His repeated forgiveness began in the Sacred Grove, when the first message of the First Vision was not apostasy nor restoration nor the Book of Mormon, but forgiveness. Joseph wrote in his 1832 account that the Lord's first words were, "Joseph [my son] thy sins are forgiven thee."[4] Throughout a lifetime of subsequent revelations the Savior often repeated the first message of the First Vision to Joseph with revelations such as "at this time your sins are forgiven you" (D&C 29:3); "whose sins are now forgiven you" (D&C 61:2); and "you are clean before me" (D&C 110:5). These frequent forgivenesses to Joseph were for repeated common sins, such as succumbing to negative peer pressure, and also for large-scale sins, such as losing the 116 manuscript pages of the Book of Lehi. Frequent mistakes, frequent repentance, and frequent forgiveness tells us something about Joseph Smith's growth as a prophet but more importantly about our Lord's frequently forgiving nature.

King Benjamin said that as we come to know the Savior we awaken to "the goodness of God . . . and his patience, and his long-suffering toward the children of men" (Mosiah 4:6).

Long-suffering could be translated as "consistently unwearied." Jesus never tires of our repeated efforts to grow and progress. The Lord is consistently unwearied as we faithfully battle to rid our problems of dishonesty, anger, pride, immorality, selfishness, addictions, and the like. He knows that the spirit is willing, but our flesh is yet weak. He is a patient parent who champions, encourages, and also corrects his spiritually young children as they learn to control their physical and spiritual faculties. *To those of us who repeatedly stumble as we strive to learn to walk as Christ did, the scrip-*

Jesus never tires of our repeated efforts to grow and progress.

tures are clear that the Lord is there, consistently unwearied, to pick us up and encourage us to try again and again and again. "Yea, and *as often as my people repent* will I forgive them their trespasses against me" (Mosiah 26:30; emphasis added).

Christ *Fully* Forgives Our Sins

Although the Lord freely and frequently forgives sins, some of us worry whether—or don't believe that—Christ will *fully* forgive our sins. Too many mistakenly view a repentant sinner like a banged-up used car, imagining there is some celestial Carfax report that always keeps a black mark by our name once we have been dinged and damaged through sin. We may go through the Creator's body shop and get a dent removed or our paint touched up and interior detailed, but we erringly think the history always remains. Saint Peter might, before he metaphorically buys us for service in the Lord's kingdom, say, "Oh, I see. You want to stand fully approved by God? Yes, yes. You're doing well now, but I see here you've had two different owners in the past. Someone who's gone through multiple marriages like that just . . . Well, you know, if you hadn't had that divorce we would look much more closely at making use of you . . ."

"Seems here like there's been some smoke in this one. I mean, you can't ever really get that stuff out, can you? Just kind of sticks. We can only have people that have been smoke- and drug-free in our fleet . . ."

"Yes, yes, you're running great now. Loving God with all your heart, might, mind, and strength and your neighbor as yourself on all cylinders. But it looks like there in 2008 you had your engine replaced because of a pornography blockage. Hmm. Don't know if we can approve of a servant with a history like that . . ."

This sort of tainted-goods thinking is inconsistent with the Lord's promise of full forgiveness and complete cleansing from sin. Nearly all scripture-reading people are familiar with Isaiah's beautiful language describing the thoroughness of Christ's cleansing power: "Though your sins be as scarlet, they shall be as white as snow; though they be red like crimson, they shall be as wool" (Isaiah 1:18). Anyone who has worked to get blood out of a white shirt or grape juice from a light carpet can appreciate the depth of this metaphor. If we believe Christ, we trust that there is no partial pardon with the Lord. He completely honors his exonerations. "There is no black mark on our right ankle that says '2008 sin' or brown stain behind our left ear that says '2010 trespass,'" Elder Tad R. Callister wrote, because of "the comprehensive cleansing power of the Atonement."[5] *Jesus's cleansing power is so comprehensive it causes celestial amnesia, being forgotten forever by the God who knows all.* "Behold, he who has repented of his sins, the same is forgiven, and I, the Lord, remember them no more" (D&C 58:42). Because of Christ, there is no sin that cannot be everlastingly erased, fully forgiven, and completely cleansed. It's in his cleansing nature and character to do so freely, frequently, and fully (*see Study Suggestion 2*).

Because of Christ, there is no sin that cannot be everlastingly erased, fully forgiven, and completely cleansed.

Attaining the Cleansing Power

How do we attain the Lord's cleansing power? To begin to address this question, let me first tell you about my wife, Cindy. As I type these words, I am looking across the living room as she neatly wraps a present for my daughter's birthday, folding the corners crisply and cleanly. I, on the other hand, am terrible at wrapping presents. My wife is also much, much better than I am at understanding and fixing machines, planning events, being organized, and handling complex finances, to name but a few. The beauty of marriage, however, is that because we joined our lives together by covenant and are one, all her many gifts become part of my life, even if I don't have them myself. It's wonderful. And the reverse is also true: My strengths (such as reaching high things because I'm 6'3") are her strengths too (she is 5'3"). She doesn't need the ladder to change the light bulb because she has me. And it's most likely we won't have late fees charged to our bills because of her. We each are blessed by the other's qualities as though they were our very own, even though they aren't.

So what do marriage and wrapping paper and light bulbs and late fees have to do with attaining the consistent cleansing power of Christ? Everything. One of the most powerful and frequent metaphors Jesus used to describe his relationship with his followers was marriage. "I am married unto you," he plainly said to the Israelites (Jeremiah 3:14). "Thy Maker is thine husband," Isaiah wrote (Isaiah 54:5). Paul reminded the Romans, "Ye should be married to another, even to him who is raised from the dead" (Romans 7:4). We became metaphorically married to the Messiah when we entered the waters of baptism and made a covenant with him, a ceremony which greatly parallels a wedding. We were dressed in white, there were witnesses, vows of faithfulness, a ceremony done by authority, and giving of gifts. We even took a new name upon us. Jesus was and is the Bridegroom, and all of us collectively as his baptismal disciples are his bride (*see Study Suggestion 3*).

If we understand the nature of this covenant marriage relationship with the Lord we should inherently understand what this covenant connection provides. *Like any marriage, when we covenant with Jesus we become an heir with him and attain access to all his gifts, powers, abilities, and virtues.*[6] His goodness becomes our goodness, his purity our purity, his holiness our holiness. This is because "in the ordinances thereof, the power of godliness is manifest . . . unto men in the flesh" (D&C 84:20–21). Jesus freely and willingly gives these gifts to his disciples—and many more, including his continual gift of cleansing. The key to our receiving these gifts is our covenant relationship with him. Without the covenant, there is not full access to his full gifts. With the covenant, they are freely, frequently, and fully given to his faithful family.

Most of us understand the basic mathematical idea of infinity, something that has no end. You cannot add to nor take away from it. Thus, $30 + \infty = \infty$. The sum isn't "infinity thirty," it's just infinity. Similarly, $60 + \infty = \infty$. Powerfully, the Book of Mormon repeatedly describes the Lord's divine offering to us as "infinite" (2 Nephi 9:7; 2 Nephi 25:16; Alma 34:10). It doesn't matter whether we are a thirty-, sixty-, or one hundred-fold offerer (see Matthew 13:8), as the Lord describes our efforts, or a third-hour, sixth-hour, or eleventh-hour laborer (see Matthew 20:1–16), or a four- or ten-talent servant (see Matthew 25:14–23). As long as we are linked with the infinite Lord, the end result is always the same: Reward. Kingdom. Heaven. Purity. The key to the equation is the +, the connection that links the thirty with the ∞, the connection we call a priesthood covenant with the Lord. You and I are not earning anything on our own merits, merely receiving loving gifts from Christ through covenant—including infinite gifts of cleansing. That is what the Lord means when he tells us, "I am able to make you holy" (D&C 60:7). That is why he told the original participants in the School of the Prophets to perform ordinances like washing of the feet so "that I may make you clean" (D&C 88:74). That is what it means to "come unto Christ, and be perfected in him" (Moroni 10:32). Because of our covenant with him we can be imperfect and yet clean. As long as we have come unto Christ, repented of our sins, and committed our life to him through ordinances such as baptism, the sacrament, and the holy temple, that cleansing blessing is ours, today, tomorrow, and forevermore.

Retaining the Cleansing Power

For covenant disciples, then, the real question is not, "How do I *attain* the Lord's continual cleansing power?" but more aptly becomes, "How do I *retain* the Lord's continual cleansing power?" That is what King Benjamin was getting at when he said to his covenant people that they—and therefore we—could "always *retain* a remission of your sins" (Mosiah 4:12; emphasis added). For a covenant disciple to ask whether he or she had access to the Lord's gift of cleansing today is like me asking my wife if I had access to her financial gifts today. The answer is as obvious as it is profound. Because of this sublime covenant truth, some protestant Christians preach that once you come unto Christ you always retain his saving grace and goodness forever. The Lord revealed, however, that "there is a possibility that man may fall from grace and depart from the living God; therefore let the church take heed" (D&C 20:32–33). I can depart from the Lord just as I can depart from my wife if I am not consistently showing heartfelt love and loyalty. Just as my spouse doesn't expect perfection from me nor I from her, we do expect loyalty to one another, manifest daily through thoughts, words, and deeds. For example, I promise my wife I will call her at least once per day. I do that most always. But, admittedly, there are a few days when I fail. When I come home there is usually a "How was your day?" followed by a lovingly pointed, "Was it too busy to call your wife?" To all the married men in the world who are reading these lines, and who want to remain happily married, we know what our response should be and shouldn't be. It should be a confession. A recognition. A commitment to do better. A phone call the next day. Chocolate. Those kind of actions help us remain married and retain oneness with our spouse. In marriage we call this an apology. In the gospel we call this repentance.

Thus, if the key to *attaining* the Lord's continual cleansing power is covenant, then the key to *retaining* his continual cleansing power is consistent repentance. The scriptures are abundantly clear on this point (see Proverbs 28:13; Luke 24:47; Helaman 5:11; D&C 1:32). Repentance is at heart coming to a realization that our actions are contrary to the Lord's desires, humbling ourselves, turning to and dedicating ourselves to him—realigning our "thoughts, beliefs, and behaviors that are not in harmony with His will."[7] It is change and growth and improvement and commitment toward God's ways, rejecting ungodliness and abhorring sin (see Romans 12:9; Alma 13:12). *Real repentance is a product of the heart. It's when we've arrived at an inner conclusion and commitment to follow Christ (see Study Suggestion 4).*

This inner commitment to follow Christ and be loyal to him, repenting when we go astray, can and should be done daily. The process of daily prayer culminated by the weekly ordinance of the sacrament provides our avenue to continually retain a remission of our sins and remain in our covenant relationship with Christ. In the morning when we rise and offer our prayers to God in the name of Christ, we offer ourselves. We are not just asking for things nor thanking for things, but more importantly committing ourselves to Christ's things. In our prayer we express devotion and love and a desire to be faithful and to be led by the Spirit in the day to follow Christ's teachings. We then go about our day, striving to be faithful to our covenant commitment, but inevitably we are mortal and fall somewhat short. God understands this. While not approving of such, he prepared for as much. Thus, at the close of the day, we approach God in prayer again, offering an accounting of our daily actions in the name of Christ. As his children and as agent representatives of his Son (we are metaphorically married to Christ and have taken his name upon us, remember), we report our actions to our Father. We confess those thoughts, words, and deeds that were out of alignment with his will. We apologize. We ask for forgiveness. We recommit to do good and be good. We again align ourselves with God. We express our love. In other words, we repent. We follow this process daily, like a spiritual circadian rhythm, committing, living, accounting, repenting, committing, living, accounting, repenting—sometimes through prayers verbalized, sometimes in the quiet recesses of the heart—allowing the Lord's cleansing power to encircle us, follow us, remain with us, so we can retain a remission of our sins.

On Sunday the Lord offers us a chance to commit to him not just in word, but in very deed, witnessing unto the Father in the name of his Son by a covenant and ordinance that we are truly one with his Son. In a sense, we are renewing our metaphorical wedding vows. We promise we are willing again to take upon us the name of Christ, always remember him, and keep his commandments. God, in turn, promises us we will always have his Spirit with us, which Spirit brings purification and sanctification to our souls (see 2 Nephi 31:17; Moroni 6:4). With this priesthood pronouncement, witnessed unto God, we are pardoned and purified from our sins each week. The sacrament renews the process of forgiveness, as President Boyd K. Packer taught: "Every Sunday when the sacrament is served, that is a ceremony to renew the process of forgiveness. . . . Every Sunday you cleanse yourself so that . . . your spirit will be clean."[8] Elder Dallin H. Oaks, directly referencing the cleansing power of Christ, summarized, "The cleansing power of our Savior's Atonement is renewed for us as we partake of the sacrament."[9]

If you and I want to always retain a remission of our sins, the key is not perfection, but dedication. God never has, and never will, expect perfection from us while we are in mortality. It's an impossibility, and he knows it. Jesus wants us to get rid of our perfectionist complex and instead develop a loyalty complex. Christ's cleansing grace is retained through loyal commitment to him, not through perfectly following him. While we strive to do his will because we love him (see John 14:15), we also show we love him when we repent for not doing his will (see Matthew 21:28–31). The Lord loves, as do our mortal spouses, a heartfelt "sorry," followed by a commitment of dedication—a process we can participate in daily in prayer, and weekly through the sacrament. Yielding our hearts to God

Jesus wants us to get rid of our perfectionist complex and instead develop a loyalty complex.

is a daily offering and receiving Christ's cleansing power is a daily blessing. In this way, we always retain a remission of our sins, in spite of our weakness, which causes our soul to rejoice. That continual cleansing justifies us before God, and participating in daily, repeated repentance over time sanctifies us through Christ (see D&C 20:30–31).

Always Rejoicing

The daily cleansing power of Christ is found through the everyday process of recognizing our own spiritual insufficiency, yet having a perfect brightness of hope in Christ's infinite capacity. We cannot, Pharisee-like, pat ourselves on the back for any relative righteousness and pretend we are part of the ninety and nine who need no repentance. However, we also cannot despair, thinking we are utterly hopeless in our repeated mortal imperfections. The one extreme denies the need for Jesus's daily cleansing power and the other extreme denies the efficacy of Jesus's cleansing power. Neither position is acceptable because neither position is true. Somewhere between the divergent paths of self-righteousness and utter hopelessness we find the way, the truth, and the life—we find Jesus. We find a divine partner who is willing to freely, frequently, and fully forgive his errant but repentant spouse.

> Somewhere between the divergent paths of self-righteousness and utter hopelessness we find the way, the truth, and the life—we find Jesus.

Humbly recognizing our daily shortcomings, yet confidently trusting his divine offering, we loyally commit to Christ by covenant, repenting daily when we go astray, and recommitting to him through weekly sacramental covenant. This process removes guilt—both of past sins and current weakness—and crushes the burden of perfectionism under the weight of eternal covenant. It allows us to live each day with a hope born of Christ and his grace that we are part of his covenant people, and through his merits and mercy we have attained and are retaining a daily remission of our sins. What joy and peace this brings! King Benjamin summarized all of this well when he said we should "always retain in remembrance, the greatness of God, and your own nothingness, and his goodness and long-suffering towards you." We should continually find ourselves "calling on the name of the Lord daily, and standing steadfastly in the faith" (Mosiah 4:11). And then, "If ye do this ye shall always rejoice, and be filled with the love of God, and always retain a remission of your sins" (Mosiah 4:12). Jesus offers this continual cleansing to us—today. The questions are: Do we believe in his divinity? Do we love him enough to covenant with him? Do we repent and recommit to him daily when we have strayed? Do we consistently witness this recommitment by covenant? If we can answer yes, the Lord offers us the infinite blessing he alone has the power to offer—the blessing of being pure, washed, white, and spotless; the blessing of letting go of guilt; the blessing of standing approved and confident before the presence of God; the blessing that comes from the cleansing power of Christ.

Further Study Suggestions: The Cleansing Power of Christ

Study Suggestion 1: Viewing ourselves as righteous or sinful

• Read D&C 82:3. What influence might that verse have on our perception of relative righteousness?

• Notice Jesus's loving phrase "one thing thou lackest . . ." to the rich young ruler who had kept all the commandments from his youth in Mark 10:21. Why would Jesus point out a weakness when there were so many apparent strengths in this young man? What does that tell us about how the Lord may work with us? Cross-reference this with what the Lord said to a newly baptized convert, William E. McLellin, in D&C 66:3.

• Read Revelation 3:17–18. What insights do these verses give to the saying, "The road to spiritual growth is found by openly and honestly analyzing the map of our sins." Is that saying true? If so, why? If not, why not?

Study Suggestion 2: Jesus's freely, frequently, and fully forgiving nature

• Read the father's words in the Parable of the Prodigal Son in Luke 15:22–24. What insight do those verses give you into Jesus's own nature?

• In church lessons we can make repentance and forgiveness out to be a long and arduous process. Is that always true? If so, how do we reconcile this concept with the quintessential example of forgiveness in the Book of Mormon—that of Alma the Younger, which took place over three days? (See Mosiah 27.) What about other examples, such as King Lamoni? His wife? King Lamoni's father? The Anti-Nephi-Lehis? Is there any example in the Book of Mormon where forgiveness wasn't freely granted by God as Christ-centered commitment took place in a person's heart? What do these examples teach you about Jesus and about repentance and forgiveness?

• Read Psalm 103:12 for a great metaphor about Jesus's ability to remove our sin far from us.

Study Suggestion 3: Married to Christ

• Study Hosea's marriage to the adulterous Gomer in Hosea 2 through the lens of Gomer representing covenant disciples and Hosea representing the Lord. Pay particular attention to Hosea 2:14–23. What do you learn about how the Lord views his covenant relationship with us, and how merciful he is?

• Read Revelation 19:7–8, paying particular attention to how the Saints, as Christ's wife, make themselves ready to reunite with Christ at the Second Coming. Compare the adorning elements of the bride with the armor of God in D&C 27:15–18.

• Study the following verses where our relationship to Jesus is placed in the context of marriage: Matthew 25:1–13; Luke 5:34; John 3:28–29; D&C 58:11. What other verses can you find that use this marriage metaphor?

Study Suggestion 4: Real repentance

• Elder Jörg Klebingat said, "No matter what your current status, the very moment you voluntarily choose honest, joyful, daily repentance by striving to simply do and be your very best, the Savior's Atonement envelops and follows you, as it were, wherever you go."[10] How can you repent daily and joyfully, centering your repentance more on promising to follow and not only on pronouncements of failure?

• Read Matthew 3:8. What do you think John the Baptist meant by the "fruits meet for repentance"? How are those different than steps of repentance? Why is checklist repentance incorrect and sometimes damning? What scriptural verses can you find where the Lord condemns the outer actions when the inner heart is not right?

• Read about the woman who was known as a sinner who anointed Jesus's feet with alabaster ointment and wiped them with her tears and hair in Luke 7:36–50. Notice how Christ forgives her sins. What do the woman's actions teach us about real repentance, especially as Jesus compares her actions to Simon the Pharisee's? Cross-reference this story to Matthew 3:8.

THE HEALING POWER
OF CHRIST

Many Christians, and many Latter-day Saints in particular, have been witness to the divine healing power of Christ in their lives or the lives of loved ones. Jesus, as the scriptures repeatedly attest, is the Great Physician, the Master Healer. There seems to be no malady that Christ cannot cure, and he continues to do so for many today. However, irrespective of personal righteousness and in spite of faithful prayers and blessings, many of us continue to suffer from physical or mental disabilities and pains. We believe and we have faith, yet the problems persist: the tumor remains, the slipped disc causes continual pain, infertility endures, and fatigue remains chronic. What then? What does the healing power of Christ offer when we aren't cured? Although mortal conditions may continue to plague us, Christ's promise of internal peace can remain regardless of external conditions. His offer to ease our burdens can be experienced today even if the burden remains. He heals even when there is no miracle cure. Because of the healing power of Christ, "Earth has no sorrow that heav'n cannot heal" ("Come, Ye Disconsolate," *Hymns*, no. 115).

Chapter 2

THE HEALING POWER OF CHRIST

The healing power of the Lord Jesus Christ . . .
is available for every affliction in mortality.
—Elder Dallin H. Oaks

Almost as a precursor for the startling accounts of healing in the pages of the gospels, the last Old Testament writer, Malachi, closed his book by prophesying that "the Sun of righteousness" will shortly "arise with healing in his wings" (Malachi 4:2). And heal he did. Everywhere Jesus went, he kindly extended his healing power, ridding afflicted passersby and other desperate seekers of various infirmities. Sequenced one after another in Matthew 8–9, Jesus healed a leper, a Roman centurion's paralyzed servant, the fever of Peter's mother-in-law, a multitude of sick persons, two men possessed of devils, a man of palsy, the woman with the issue of blood, raised Jairus's daughter from the dead, gave sight to two blind men, and healed a man who was dumb. In total, that's ten miraculous healings, all of which took place over what appears to be two days of our Lord's ministry. If that doesn't impress, consider that there are only fourteen recorded healings mentioned in all of the Old Testament, and just five in the entire Book of Mormon (*see Study Suggestion 1*). *More than 1,500 scriptural pages and 5,000 years of*

God's dealings with his children chronicle about twenty healings. Jesus halved that in two days and two pages. Matthew concludes these two healing-filled days with "and Jesus went about all the cities and villages, teaching . . . preaching . . . and healing every sickness and every disease among the people" (Matthew 9:35), lumping yet even more healings into that sweeping statement. His pen couldn't even keep up.

These miraculous healings by the power of Christ continue today. A 2008 Pew Forum survey of 32,913 Americans found that 36 percent of those surveyed had "experienced or witnessed a divine healing." The group with the highest percentage were Latter-day Saints, with 69 percent of them saying they had been part of a divine healing, and between 50 to 60 percent of other Christians expressing the same.[1] If you were to look around an LDS congregation of roughly 200 people, odds are about 140 of them have seen Christ's modern-day healing hand in action. From a variety of denominations there are literally thousands upon thousands of accounts of divine healing through faith in Christ. Can you imagine if we compiled all of them into one book? Like Saint Matthew, we modern believers could sweepingly say, "And Jesus's healing power continued throughout every nation, kindred, tongue, and people, healing all manner of diseases and sicknesses in the latter days" (*see Study Suggestion 2*).

When Physical Healing Doesn't Occur

While the Lord's power to miraculously heal physical infirmities is experienced by thousands, sometimes we or our loved ones are *not* physically healed. We have faith, we pray with real intent, we humble ourselves, we seek priesthood blessings, we place names on temple rolls, but the malady remains. We wonder: "Why didn't the healing blessing work? Did I not have *enough* faith? Does God not love me as he loves others he has healed? Have I done something wrong?" I have asked myself similar questions in some of the unhealed physical problems I have personally experienced or seen loved ones endure. Why does he sometimes not heal?

Because Jesus seemed to heal everyone in the gospels every time, sometimes when we ask the Lord to be physically healed we assume it should happen no matter what. But that's a bit like a foreigner learning about America on a holiday: It can create unrealistic assumptions. A friend of mine from another country first visited the United States on Halloween and saw that everyone who knocked on any door got candy. What an awesome country! He assumed from what he saw that it happened every day for every American child. He didn't understand that Halloween was a special event and not an everyday occurrence. *Similarly, physical healings are not handed out each time we knock on God's door and ask for them, in spite of what we may deduce from the spiritual festival of the gospels.* The Lord will heal according to the persons' faith and the Father's will, but as we become more mature in our Christianity we become less demanding of an automatic fix. We gain better perspective about why sometimes bodily healing isn't granted (*see Study Suggestion 3*). We understand that disease and death—including untimely occurrences—are a necessary part of God's work and glory, and to heal every hurt upon every asking would counteract the eternal purposes of God. As the Lord himself said, unless the seed of the body dies and is planted into the ground you cannot have the fruit of resurrection spring forth from it (see John 12:23–24). Sometimes physical healings don't happen because there is something to learn from the suffering or the death of a loved one. Sometimes these infirmities give us a purer and deeper faith, a faith that, as a father who lost his teenage daughter to cancer once said, "is in Jesus Christ and is not dependent on outcomes."[2]

Therefore, in spite of the fact that many of us will experience the miracle of Christ's healing in our lifetimes, inevitably each of us will also have the equally important experience of Jesus withholding that physical healing hand. After all, the woman with the issue of blood surely suffered from later challenges. Lazarus died a second time. We must all suffer through unhealed mortal debilitations, as it won't be until our bodies are resurrected that Jesus performs his "consummate act of healing," as Elder Russell M. Nelson called it.[3] Until then, however, what healing can Christ offer for someone who remains infirm? What does Jesus do when it appears that removing our sickness or disability is not part of God's will and we are "appointed unto" certain ailments? (See D&C 42:48.) How can we experience the everyday healing power of Christ if we are not cured?

Healing as Wholeness

To understand how Christ can offer his power of healing today regardless of whether someone's physical infirmity remains may require us to redefine our understanding of healing and therefore reimagine what is meant by Christ's everyday healing power. Dr. Wendy Ulrich's explanation can help:

"Let me first distinguish between healing from cure. Cure returns us to our previous state of wellness, which is usually what we long for. But the scriptures never speak of the gift of cure. They speak of the gift of healing. Healing is a different process from cure. Healing involves a spiritual and emotional reweaving of our life story to incorporate, not merely remove, our injuries. It involves growth and personal change, maturation into a new state of deeper trust in God despite, not in the absence of, suffering."[4]

Thus, in spite of uncured physical difficulties we can yet experience the miracle of healing. Perhaps a real-life example can best illustrate this not-cured-yet-healed concept.

Michele Reyes, in the January 2013 *Ensign*, wrote about her experiences in a story titled "Whole Enough." As a teenager, she was involved in a car accident that took most of her left arm. The experience changed her forever, giving her "an opportunity to witness the power of the Atonement in a unique way."[5]

Her life today revolves around her family, around her roles of wife and mother, which she loves. Before she had children, though, she worried about some things most of us might not. How would she manage making dinner? Or any of the other daily tasks that a mother of young children accomplishes without a second thought? At the time she wrote her story, she was the mother of five children, and the difference she thought would be a hindrance had become instead "a symbol of love." Her children don't usually notice that she's physically different from other mothers. In fact, she says that what remains of her arm "is a source of comfort for my children to hold when they cry or fall asleep at night. . . . I see it as evidence of the Savior's ability to create something good out of something tragic."[6]

She talks about how her outlook has been transformed from trepidation to acceptance, seeing her life now as a work in progress. She sees that the experience she's having as a mother highlights how the Atonement can work in her life every day, writing: "I have felt the Atonement already begin to heal me. . . . I feel the Atonement working in my life *now*. I have realized that the healing power need not begin only when the Resurrection occurs. The wholeness has already begun when, every night, one of my children tenderly holds what remains of my arm and slips into slumber. . . . I have decided that, for now, I am as whole as I need to be."[7]

Michele's story is a healing miracle, just as potent and real as a bodily cure. We see evidence of God giving an inner healing to her heart and soul, an internal peace overcoming external trouble. Inner healing comes to us through God providing miraculous spiritual gifts such as increased patience, understanding, strength, empathy, and love. In the midst of our sufferings God touches our hearts and applies the balm of Gilead to what's festering inside despite our circumstances on the outside. These spiritual gifts penetrate deep into the tissues of our wounded soul and enable a healing through oneness with God.

Inner healing comes to us through God providing miraculous spiritual gifts such as increased patience, understanding, strength, empathy, and love.

One word the scriptures use often to describe this type of internal, spiritual healing is the word *wholeness. Wholeness is a unity between body, mind, spirit, and God. Wholeness aligns with God and accepts "Thy will be done" sincerely.*

Wholeness says that although we have an uncured physical limitation or pain or problem, our heart has become softened, our spirit attuned to God's Spirit, our faith fortified, and something sweet from heaven above has whispered peace to our troubled soul. Jesus promised all his

The world can
sometimes give us
cures, but Christ
can always give
us wholeness.

followers this healing gift when he said to his Apostles: "Peace I leave with you, my peace I give unto you: not as the world giveth, give I unto you. Let not your heart be troubled, neither let it be afraid" (John 14:27). The world can sometimes give us cures, but Christ can always give us wholeness.

This concept of wholeness is exemplified in the story of the ten lepers. All ten were healed physically, but only the one Samaritan who came back and gave thanks did the Lord pronounce as being "whole" (Luke 17:19). The Lord used that same phrase with Enos, when he had repented of his sins. "Thy faith hath made thee whole" (Enos 1:8), the Lord proclaimed, implying an internal healing—spirit-centered, not bodily. Enos and the Samaritan leper had achieved a peace with God—a unity of body, mind, and spirit, and with it a deeper, more lasting healing.

Spiritual Healing Today

One beautiful aspect of understanding healing as wholeness is that we begin to see how we can each be influenced today through the healing power of Christ. We can—and should—seek his healing power through medicine and blessings to cure infirmities, but more importantly we should seek Jesus's healing power for our souls. We let his love and mercy and tenderness come upon us. We let the Lord teach us what he would have us learn and feel from our present situation and what he would have us do. We let him align our hearts with God and give us peace. We let him help make us whole. This type of healing allows Christ's divinity into a broader spectrum of daily infirmities beyond mere physical health, one which includes the healing of our minds, emotions, hearts, and spirits (*see Study Suggestion 4*). Jesus spoke of this type of spiritual healing often: "Will ye not now return unto me, and repent of your sins, and be converted, that I may heal you?" he asked (3 Nephi 9:13; see also Matthew 13:15; 3 Nephi 18:32; D&C 112:13).

This concept of spiritual healing is evident in the situation of my friend and neighbor Emily. Emily developed a debilitating chronic illness after her full-time LDS mission. She has since endured years of difficulty and pain without being cured physically, to the point that she said, "I have forgotten what it feels like to be healthy." But notice how Christ continues to heal her today even when her malady remains. She writes:

"I lean on the Lord for support and guidance in my illness all the time. It is inspiring to feel the impressions of the Holy Ghost and know that Heavenly Father is teaching me. Through the gift of the Holy Ghost, He gives me peace, love, and assurance. I know by these specific impressions that I am of worth. Even if some days all I am able to do is lie in bed and pray that the pain lessens, it is comforting to know that He cares.

"As a result of my trials, I am learning a powerful truth—I am a child of God. Now, instead of feeling empty and alone, I am filled with His love."[8]

This concept of spiritual healing is always available, miraculously addressing the source of pain often without removing the physical problem itself. *What goes on outside might continue, but what goes on inside is drastically changed.* Physical grief is transformed into a life of gratitude. Frustration is overwhelmed by the heavenly gift of patience. Bitterness is soothed by the divine endowment of acceptance. The prayer of faith is answered with the healing blessing of peace. Through the influence of the Holy Ghost, wholeness is given: a gift of oneness and unity with God through body, mind, and spirit—a healing that can influence a believer daily and last much, much longer than a healed joint or cell, sinew, or bone. Is that not miraculous? Thus, consistently and profoundly, Christ heals us even if he does not cure us. This healing blessing can be ours today if we seek it in faith.

Christ heals us, even if he does not cure us.

Receiving the Healing Power: Faith

So how do we unleash this everyday healing power of Christ? One word: Faith. "Thy faith hath made thee whole" (Matthew 9:22) was said so often by the Lord that President Spencer W. Kimball said the phrase "almost became a chorus."[9] Jesus performed healing miracles upon "seeing their faith" (Matthew 9:2). "O woman, great is thy faith" (Matthew 15:28), he said to the Canaanite before her daughter was made whole. The prophet Moroni concluded that the Lord "worketh by power, according to the faith of the children of men" (Moroni 10:7). Literally hundreds of similar scriptures and prophetic quotes could fill these pages. But what do the scriptures and prophets—and the Lord himself—mean by "have faith"? What does that actually look like in reality, today, to seek healing in faith? *True to the Faith* informs us, "Faith is much more than passive belief. You express your faith through action—by the way you live."[10] Like a young child who shows his trust by jumping into his father's arms from the side of the pool, we show our faith in Christ through actions that demonstrate our trust in God. The following are six faith-based actions that we can do to help receive the daily healing power of Christ in our lives:

1. Be obedient. As Jesus taught us with the man born blind (see John 9:2–3), iniquity normally doesn't cause infirmity.[11] However, disobedience can affect our ability to be healed and made whole by the Redeemer. If healing is wholeness, and wholeness is oneness with God, then disbelief and disobedience disrupt wholeness and healing. Jesus was never stumped by difficult problems, only by difficult hearts. In his own town of Nazareth, "*he could there do no mighty work*, save that he laid his hands upon a few sick folk, and healed them. And he marvelled because of their unbelief" (Mark 6:5–6; emphasis added). On another occasion Jesus lamented that "this people's heart is waxed gross . . . lest at any time they . . . should be converted, and I should heal them" (Matthew 13:15).

Mormon tells us that among his own people, "Wickedness did prevail upon the face of the whole land . . . and the work of miracles and of healing did cease because of the iniquity of the people" (Mormon 1:13). *Humility and obedience are the prerequisites for fully receiving Christ's healing balm.* Elder Richard G. Scott of the Twelve said: "Act now to avail yourself of the healing power of the Atonement of Jesus Christ. I testify that your faith and obedience will assure that He will help you."[12] If and when disobedience occurs, then let us repent to help healing happen (see Jeremiah 3:22). As we

Jesus was never stumped by difficult problems, only by difficult hearts.

submit to the Lord through striving to follow his teachings, the Holy Ghost will deliver the healing effects of Christ's Atonement.

2. *Be prayerful.* Prayer is an inseparable act of faith related to both spiritual and physical healing because sincere prayer aligns us with God. As a well-known hymn asks us, "Ere you left your room this morning, / Did you think to pray? / . . . When your soul was full of sorrow, / Balm of Gilead did you borrow / At the gates of day?"[13] One of the few physical healings in the Old Testament—Hezekiah's life being extended by fifteen years—was the result of faithful prayer. The Lord said to Hezekiah, "I have heard thy prayer, I have seen thy tears: behold, I will heal thee" (2 Kings 20:5). Elder Shane Bowen of the Seventy, speaking in general conference about his struggles with his young son's tragic death, said, "As I felt the guilt, anger, and self-pity trying to consume me, I prayed that my heart could change. Through very personal sacred experiences, the

Lord gave me a new heart. . . . I have learned that the bitter, almost unbearable pain can become sweet as you turn to your Father in Heaven and plead for His comfort."[14] As you pray, ask your Father in humility to teach you and help you learn his will. When taken in multiple doses daily, prayer becomes a powerful healing medicine to both body and spirit.

3. *Be blessed through the priesthood.* This is perhaps the most well-known act of faith when we need healing: to seek after a faithful Melchizedek Priesthood holder to administer a formal blessing. The very petition for such a blessing—demonstrating belief in Jesus Christ and his restored priesthood power—unlocks the healing power of Christ. James admonishes us, "Is any among you afflicted? let him pray. . . . Is any sick among you? let him call for the elders of the church; and let them pray over him, anointing him with oil in the name of the Lord: And the prayer of faith shall save the sick" (James 5:13–15). The Doctrine and Covenants tells us, "And the elders of the church, two or more, shall be called, and shall pray for and lay their hands upon them in my name" (D&C 42:44). The oil with which we are anointed represents Jesus Christ's Atonement and signifies his healing power.[15] When that oil is administered and received by those who have faith, it facilitates the internal and external healing power of Christ, regardless of the words that are or are not spoken by the one sealing the anointing (*see Study Suggestion 5*).[16]

4. *Be active in worship.* Attending church, studying the scriptures, and participating in the temple connect us to the healing powers of Christ through his holy word and holy ordinances. The prophet Jacob tells us that the scriptures and the words of the

prophets contain "the pleasing word of God, yea, the word which healeth the wounded soul" (Jacob 2:8). The Lord requested all to participate in congregational worship so they can be healed: "Nevertheless, ye shall not cast him out of your synagogues, or your places of worship, for unto such shall ye continue to minister; for ye know not but what they will return and repent, and come unto me with full purpose of heart, and I shall heal them" (3 Nephi 18:32). Connected to worshipping at Church is a relationship with the Lord's local agent, the bishop (or branch president), who Elder David A. Bednar said "is the spiritual physician's assistant who is authorized to help you repent and heal."[17] And ultimately, the Lord's holy house is a house of healing. Hezekiah's people were healed because of their temple worship (see 2 Chronicles 30:15–20), and we can be as well. There is an unmistakable application in Ezekiel's vision of waters flowing out from under the Jerusalem temple eastward and healing the Dead Sea: "These waters issue out toward the east country, and go down into the desert, and go into the sea: which being brought forth into the sea, the waters shall be healed. And it shall come to pass, that every thing that liveth, which moveth, whithersoever the rivers shall come, shall live" (Ezekiel 47:8–9). In the Lord's temple, as names are placed on sacred temple rolls, we can pray for others and be prayed for ourselves, be sanctified and blessed through holy ordinances, learn of God's plans and purposes, and partake more fully of God's divine healing spirit.

5. *Be patient.* The process of physical, emotional, mental, and spiritual healing is often slow. It usually takes time to put difficult pieces together into a cohesive wholeness. The modern prophets teach us: "The process of healing may take time. Trust in the Savior.

He will heal you and give you peace."[18] Speaking of spiritual healing, Elder David A. Bednar said, "Serious spiritual wounds require sustained treatment and time to heal completely and fully."[19] Doses of divine healing, like answers to prayers, are scheduled according to God's prescriptions, not our mortal orders. Healing from God, like revelation, happens "in [God's] own time, and in his own way, and according to his own will" (D&C 88:68). As Elder Neal A. Maxwell taught, faith in God also implies faith in his timing,[20] which faith also applies to patience with the process of healing through Christ.

> Doses of divine healing, like answers to prayers, are scheduled according to God's prescriptions, not our mortal orders.

6. *Be still.* If true healing is wholeness—a oneness with God in mind, body, and spirit—then healing can take place only as we obey the scriptural injunction to "be still, and know that [he is] God" (Psalm 46:10; see also D&C 101:16).[21] Learn to be quiet and to listen to his Spirit. When you pray, instead of only asking God to cure you, ask him also to teach you. If a physical illness or pain yet remains, let him instruct you how to respond to the pain with grace. Let him whisper peace to your mind, comfort to your soul, and show you how to navigate your day-to-day life with the disability. *Most often you can't be cured just by trying harder. But you can be made whole by being softer.* Remember that your progress is not measured in the *doing* but in the *becoming.* Not in release from pain, but in accepting his will. Not in being more physically capable as others are, but in being more spiritually sensitive as the Lord is.

Offer your whole soul to him, and he will offer wholeness of your soul to you. Jesus tells us to "learn of me, and listen to my words; walk in the meekness of my Spirit, and you shall have peace in me" (D&C 19:23). Learn + listen + walk = peace. Being still helps us to let Jesus heal our soul and make it whole in his own divine way.

The Healing of the Nations

As evidenced in the gospels, Jesus was sent to heal, in rates and ratios perhaps never manifest before or since on earth. His divine physical healings continue today, as seen in the lives and testimonies of many of his believers. Although miraculous bodily cures do not always happen, Christ offers spiritual healing to each of his disciples on a daily basis—a wholeness that comes from a unity with God through body, mind, and spirit. Through his divinity, Christ gives healing by providing patience, sending strength, accelerating acceptance, unveiling understanding, and giving eyes to see, ears to hear, and hearts to feel. He gives his divine gift of peace even when our troubles remain. This spiritual healing lasts even when physical problems persist or return. Thus, Jesus can consistently heal us even if he doesn't yet cure us. The healing power of Christ is available daily to treat every mortal affliction, whether physical, emotional, mental, or spiritual. We receive this healing power through our manifestations of faith in Christ: obedience, prayer, priesthood blessings, personal worship, patience, and being still, among others.

Ultimately, these faithful actions lead us to the Tree of Life, which tree represents Jesus (see 1 Nephi 11:8–24). This tree not only provides us the fruit of the Love of God, but, often overlooked, the fruit's growing companion: its leaves. And what do

Through his divinity, Christ gives healing by providing patience, sending strength, accelerating acceptance, unveiling understanding, and giving eyes to see, ears to hear, and hearts to feel. He gives his divine gift of peace even when our troubles remain.

those leaves on the Tree of Life offer us? John the Revelator tells us: "And the leaves of the tree were for the healing of the nations" (Revelation 22:2). The fruit of the love of God is often wrapped up in the leaves of Christ's healing power of which we can consistently partake as he lovingly provides us healing in our everyday lives. As he anciently reminded Moses, so he reminds each of us today: "I am the Lord that healeth thee" (Exodus 15:26).

Further Study Suggestions: The Healing Power

Study Suggestion 1: Healings in the Old Testament and Book of Mormon

• As noted, in my study of the scriptures I counted fourteen recorded healings in the Old Testament and five in the Book of Mormon. Listed are some of these healings. What connections, patterns, and themes do you see in them that brought to pass Christ's physical healing power?

The Old Testament: Sarah (Genesis 18); Miriam (Numbers 12); Hannah (1 Samuel 1); Naaman (2 Kings 5); Hezekiah (2 Kings 20; see also Isaiah 38).

The Book of Mormon: Zeezrom (Alma 15); Nephi raising his brother from the dead (3 Nephi 7); Nephi casting out devils and healing sickness (3 Nephi 7); Jesus healing the multitudes (3 Nephi 17); the disciples of Jesus healing the sick, raising the dead, and causing the blind to see and the lame to walk (4 Nephi 1).

Study Suggestion 2: Christ's continued power to heal

• When Moses complained to the Lord that his speech impediment would make it difficult to command Pharaoh to let Israel go, the Lord linked his creative and healing power together in one doctrinally pointed question: "Who hath made man's mouth?" (Exodus 4:11). How is Jesus's continued healing power linked to his creative power? Study Genesis 3:19; Acts 7:50; Helaman 12:8; D&C 38:8; and Moses 1:4 to learn some potential reasons why.

• Many people from other faiths are healed through Christ, as mentioned in the 2008 Pew Forum study. How is that possible when they aren't blessed by a Melchizedek Priesthood holder? Study the story in Mark 9:38–40. What insight does Christ provide? Why should we be blessed by a Melchizedek Priesthood holder if healing can be given through non-priesthood means as a gift of the Spirit? (See D&C 46:19–20.)

Study Suggestion 3: Why physical healing sometimes isn't granted

• If physical healing isn't always God's will, then why does he sometimes provide it? Read the following accounts for insights into how Jesus's healing power furthered his more important work regarding his divine role as the Redeemer of mankind: Matthew 9:1–8; Luke 8:2–3; John 9:1–3; 11:14–15. See also how the Lord's "fame" was spread through his healings in Matthew 4:24; 9:25–26, 30–31; Mark 1:27–28; Luke 5:13–15.

Study Suggestion 4: Spiritual, mental, physical, emotional healing

• Study the healing accounts in Matthew 12:15 and Luke 6:19. What do you think it means that Jesus "healed them *all*"? Was everyone in those congregations of thousands physically infirm? Study the account of healing in 3 Nephi 17:7. What evidence is there that the healings Jesus provided were more than physical?

• Study the healing of the epileptic boy in Mark 9:14–29. Notice that the father of the boy pled for Jesus to "have compassion on *us*, and help *us*" (Mark 9:22; emphasis added). How can Christ's healing power heal those who struggle with the daily disabilities and pains of loved ones?

Study Suggestion 5: Priesthood blessings of healing

• Study Elder Dallin H. Oaks's talk "Healing the Sick" (*Ensign*, May 2010, 47–50). In this talk Elder Oaks outlines multiple factors that are involved in a person being healed by priesthood power. He outlines five factors: anointing, sealing the anointing, faith, the words of the blessing, and the will of the Lord. What do you learn about those five factors from Elder Oaks's talk? Although he is primarily speaking about physical healing, how do his insights relate to the concept of healing as wholeness in this chapter? What do you learn?

THE RESTORING POWER
OF CHRIST

There is no way around it—life is not fair. Each day, through no fault of their own, people are falsely accused, oppressed, hurt, or abused by others. Some are cruelly robbed of things they hold dear: their good name, loved ones, financial security, mental and physical abilities. Yet others are denied opportunities they long for and deserve: freedom, education, health, family, marriage, and children. Since the Fall of Adam and Eve the world's equity meter has been thrown off-kilter—and is completely broken for some. In his goodness, however, God sent his Son, Jesus Christ, to make at-one-ment for his children to bring things into harmony—an offering of rebalancing, restitution, recompense, and restoration. Jesus's divine gift not only restores purity to the sinner and life to the dead, but also restores capacity to the incapacitated, love to the lonely, family to the solitary, and opportunity to the oppressed. Whether in this life or the next, Jesus will fully restore and then some. This recompensing reality enables Christ's followers to freely forgive, bear suffering with patience, be confidently meek, and enjoy the assurance of hope. "Therefore," we learn in scripture, be "merciful unto your brethren; deal justly, judge righteously, and do good continually; and if ye do all these things then shall ye receive your reward; yea, ye shall have mercy restored unto you again; ye shall have justice restored unto you again; ye shall have a righteous judgment restored unto you again; and ye shall have good rewarded unto you again. For that which ye do send out shall return unto you again, and be restored" (Alma 41:13–15). This is the restoring power of Christ.

Chapter 3

THE RESTORING POWER OF CHRIST

Someday God will enlarge the miracle
of Easter to cosmic scale.

—Phillip Yancey

There is a grand lesson to learn from a light bulb. On December 17, 2010, a lit 300-watt light bulb was mistakenly left on top of a wooden speaker enclosure in the attic of the Provo (Utah) Tabernacle. Within a few hours, unstoppable flames had consumed the interior of the historic 125-year-old building built by Mormon pioneers, causing fifteen million dollars in damage and leaving nothing but a five-brick-wide exterior shell. The tabernacle had served for more than a century as a place for gathering, conferences, performances, speeches, and events, and was a beautiful architectural sight in the heart of Provo's city center. Now it was nothing but a heap of burnt rubble. What a tragedy. However, nearly a year later, in his opening remarks of general conference on October 1, 2011, President Thomas S. Monson announced that the burnt Provo Tabernacle would be restored—and not just as a tabernacle, but as a temple. An audible exuberance was heard throughout the congregation at the announcement, and not just because Provo would be getting their second temple. The magic in the announcement was because something that seemed to have been tragically lost was going to be given back. What was burnt and dead was going to be wiped clean and given life. What was broken was going to be fixed. Something taken was to be restored—this time with an angel Moroni on the spire.

The story of the Provo City Center Temple serves as a microscopic example of a cosmic force in our lives—the divine power of restoration. On this earth you and I suffer the effects of a fallen world. Plucked from our Heavenly Parents' premortal fireside, we are sent to this earth with all its stark contrasts of health and sickness, peace and war, joy and pain, good and evil. God our Father takes good notes of the things we experience in mortality. He who notices the fall of every sparrow and the loss of every hair (see Matthew 10:29–31) keeps an exact inventory. As a loving Father he weeps when we suffer, particularly when our sufferings and problems come from situations not of our choosing—when a 300-watt bulb burns through our wooden life—our parents divorce, our spouse betrays us, someone accuses us falsely, we experience a physical or mental debilitation, we suffer oppression, poverty, violence, or taste the bitterness of a child's untimely death. For some, these mortal burns don't just singe their faith in God—the flames completely gut their house of faith.

In the midst of the telestial burns we suffer, however, stands the celestial figure of Christ, who says to you and me, "Your life is in my hands. In my own way, and in my own time, I will redeem. I will restore." God, through his Son, Jesus Christ, offers each of us *complete* redemption—not just from sin and death, but all-out redemption from the wrongs of this fallen world. Jesus's divine offering has power to make at one all things that are currently undone. "We have seen the lives of loved ones—and maybe our own—figuratively burned to the ground," said Sister Linda Reeves, second counselor in the Relief Society general presidency, "and have wondered why a loving and caring Heavenly Father would allow such things to happen. But He does not leave us in the ashes."[1] Because of the

Jesus's divine offering has power to make at one all things that are currently undone.

Savior's restoring power all mortal burns will be healed, corrected, made right, rebuilt, and restored—and then yes, more: with an angel on top. That power can, and should, change everything.

The Solution: At-one-ment through Christ

Jesus came to redeem men from *all* the effects of the Fall of Adam and Eve. Although the Fall was necessary for God's purposes, paradise was lost. Murders were committed. Sin became common among men. Innocents suffered. The wicked prospered. Healthy cells metastasized. Families fractured. The quiet, balanced harmony in Eden shattered (*see Study Suggestion 1*). Therefore, God offered to make things right—he offered atonement through his Son. The ultimate definition of "the word *atone* means to reconcile, or to restore to harmony."[2] We owe this intimate yet infinitely beautiful English scriptural word to William Tyndale, who connected it to Jesus's suffering and passion when, in the sixteenth century, he translated Romans 5:11 into English as, "And not only so, but we also joy in God through our Lord Jesus Christ, by whom we have now received the atonement."[3] If we break the word down into three parts as "at–one–ment," we can more clearly understand what is meant by the idea: to take what is out of harmony and make it "at one" again, or brought back to its proper, balanced, rightful state.

When we speak of Jesus and his restoring Atonement we readily see the implications of being reconciled to God regarding sin: Because of our disobedience we are out of harmony with the purity and glory of God (see Romans 3:23), and thus need to be cleansed, redeemed, reconciled, and made at-one with our Father. This balancing of the celestial scales is made possible by Jesus's voluntary sacrifice for sin, which paid our debt and gave us his holiness if we will receive him—"The Great Exchange," as Christian theologians have explained it (see Chapter 1, The Cleansing Power). Paul says, "God, who hath reconciled us to himself by Jesus Christ . . . hath made him to be sin for us, who knew no sin" (2 Corinthians 5:18, 21). This spiritual reconciliation to God by virtue of Christ's offering is the central premise of all Christianity.

Aside from the divine mercy of reconciling our sin, Jesus's exercise of his restoring power is also made manifest profoundly in the glorious truth of a universal resurrection. Each person ever born on earth will one day be raised to immortal glory as a free gift of restoring grace from the Lord (see John 5:28–29; 1 Corinthians 15:22). Why does Jesus promise to do this? Partly because losing our physical body to death is an inherited effect of the Fall, and thus Christ promises full restoration of life to all who lose this bodily gift. Also inherited from the Fall are flawed aspects of mortal bodies such as having a bad knee or asthma, losing your hair, being uncoordinated or physically weak. Much more serious are debilitations such as type 1 diabetes, chronic fatigue, depression, cancer, Alzheimer's, and a host of other bodily sicknesses and problems.

Whatever the physical shortcoming or challenge, each of us has or will experience many of them. But what does the power of restoration say? It says that bodily imperfections and death are results of a fallen world. They are outcomes of Eden. *Thus, as part of his at-one-ment Jesus will resurrect and restore us to bodily immortality, glorious beauty, and perfect physical capacity.* Those who are missing an arm or a leg will have them restored. Those who cannot walk or run will one day know how an Olympic sprinter feels. Those who suffer from mental handicaps will one day be restored with fully functioning and infinite cerebral capacity. To counteract the Fall, Christ will restore our bodies to a pristine, perfect, immortal state (see D&C 138:17). So pristine, in fact, that Elder James E. Talmage said: "Mortal eye cannot see nor mind comprehend the beauty, glory, and majesty of a righteous woman made perfect in the celestial kingdom of God."[4] The same promise undoubtedly applies to righteous men. The restoring power of Christ promises us that "the soul shall be restored to the body, and the body to the soul; yea, and every limb and joint shall be restored to its body; yea, even a hair of the head shall not be lost; but all things shall *be restored to their proper and perfect frame.* And now, my son, this is the restoration of which has been spoken by the mouths of the prophets—and then shall the righteous shine forth in the kingdom of God" (Alma 40:23–25; emphasis added). Or as Paul said to the Philippians, Jesus will "change our vile body, that it may be fashioned like unto his glorious body" (Philippians 3:21). For those who have dealt with the difficulty of physical or mental debilitation or the indescribable loss of a loved one, I cannot think of scriptures that should produce more gratitude for our Lord and his restoring power than those verses.

Jesus Can Perfectly Right *Every* Mortal Wrong

The effects of the Fall of Adam and Eve also include a multiplicity of factors besides sin and death, such as poverty, suffering, oppression, and so forth. Thus, the full concept of Jesus's restoring power involves the power of rebalancing everything that is a result of the Fall to an at-one status. That's right, everything (*see Study Suggestion 2*). In his own time and in his own way, all the imbalanced inherited effects of Eden—including injustice, inequity, and unfairness—will be made right through the perfect, all-encompassing atoning power of Christ. Elder Richard G. Scott taught, "The Atonement will not only help us overcome our transgressions and mistakes, but in His time, it will resolve all inequities of life—those things that are unfair which are the consequences of circumstance or others' acts and not our own decisions."[5] *Whether in this life or the next Christ will repay, reinstate, renew, refresh, or return any blessing that was lost, denied, or taken in this life. He will perfectly restore, rectify, redeem, and recompense any injustice or undue suffering that was a result of our mortal experience.*

Christ's power of restoration says, "If you didn't have the opportunity to be married in this life, you will eventually. If you couldn't bear children, you'll be given that blessing. If you lost a child to an untimely death, you'll have them back and raise them. If you've been denied a physical capacity, you'll one day regain it.

If you've never had the opportunity to hear the gospel in this life, you'll be given that in full" (*see Study Suggestion 3*). Joseph Smith, in wonderful, prophetic power taught: "All your losses will be made up to you in the resurrection, provided you continue faithful. By the vision of the Almighty I have seen it."[6] This is because the central feature of Christ's Atonement is to perfectly right every mortal wrong. When the full effect of the Atonement is unleashed in a person's life, it takes what was undone by mortality and restores it into its divinely intended condition. In his holy time and way, Jesus will fully restore and then some. President Boyd K. Packer summarized: "Restoring what you cannot restore, healing the wound you cannot heal, fixing that which you broke and you cannot fix is the very purpose of the atonement of Christ."[7] That is what Jesus does: he brings balance. That is what Jesus promises: full recompense. That is who Jesus is: The Restorer.

> The central feature of Christ's Atonement is to perfectly right every mortal wrong.

Christ's Virtues: What Restoration Restores in Us

The truth of Jesus's wide-ranging restoring power can and should fill our lives with the gift of hope, greatly influencing our daily attitudes and behavior, giving us power to be more Christlike in our day-to-day efforts to follow the Lord's teachings. Take forgiveness, for example. Suppose something has been taken from us that we want back—our good name, peace, health, an opportunity, a job, a relationship, you name it. Our natural inclination is to seek revenge or immediately demand the return of what was lost. However, things that are unfairly taken are rarely recovered quickly. The problem is compounded because what was taken often cannot possibly be returned by those who have taken it. What mortal can give back a life? A good name? Someone's self-worth? Their purity? Their peace of mind? This is part of what makes forgiving once so hard, let alone seventy times seven (see Matthew 18:21–22). How can I forgive when the person who's offended me can't pay restitution? How can I ever reclaim what was lost? If I can't reclaim it from them, how can I forgive? The answer is in restoration. A mother's counsel to her teenager explains this principle perfectly.

I still remember where I was when I heard that Elizabeth Smart—the fourteen-year-old LDS girl who had been abducted at knifepoint from her home on the upper bench of Salt Lake City—had been found alive after nine months of captivity at the hands of two homeless persons. Over the weeks, months, and years that followed, details of her horrific ordeal came to light. Forced into a polygamous marriage on the first night she was abducted, she spent the next nine months suffering unimaginable terror, brutality, depravation, starvation, abuse, and daily rape. The pages of her book *My Story* give a glimpse into the hell she suffered. When she was finally found and reunited with her parents, Elizabeth Smart's mother said to her about her captors: "[They have] taken nine months of your life that you will never get back again. . . . You may never feel like justice has been served or that true restitution has been made. But you don't need to worry about that. At the end of the day, God . . . will make up to you every pain and loss that you have suffered."[8] When I read that sublime parental teaching,

I couldn't help but see how the divine power of restoration was at work in allowing Elizabeth Smart to let go of the unimaginable injustices she suffered. Restoration not only helped her let go but also helped her forgive. Elizabeth said: "I believe that God not only suffered for me, but that He will make everything up to me in His own time and His own way. That gives me the peace I need to feel like justice will win out in the end. *That is why I could eventually forgive my captors.*"9

In another example, a Latter-day Saint woman whose daughter, Kaylee, had been emotionally abused by a teacher wrote the following that illustrates this same restorative principle: "I found hope in the Prophet Joseph's exhortation to 'lay hold of' hope in Christ and the joy that we anticipate in the Resurrection, for as Joseph Smith said, 'What can [these disasters] do? Nothing. *All your losses will be made up to you* in the resurrection, provided you continue faithful' [*Teachings of Presidents of the Church: Joseph Smith* (2007), 51]. As I read that last sentence, understanding came: The Lord would make up *all* my losses, *all* of Kaylee's losses. I no longer needed to be angry. I no longer needed to mourn. Because of Him—because He would restore all that I'd lost—I could forgive! My heart surged with hope, and I smiled through tears of gratitude."10 Because of Christ's restoring power, we can be merciful and forgiving, and let injustices and offenses go out of our heart as we turn to the Redeemer, instead of exacting it from others, for recompense.

In Joel 2:25 the word *I* is important; God says, "*I* will restore to you the years that the locust hath eaten, the cankerworm, and the caterpiller, and the palmerworm." The person who has dealt us an injustice may not want to—or be able to—ever recompense us. *But Jesus's restoring hands are both willing and able, and opening our hands to God's makes it easier to unclench our fists towards others.* I've often marveled at how Christ himself could so calmly and patiently endure his injustices: being spit upon, buffeted, beaten, and afflicted, yet he "opened not his mouth" (Isaiah 53:7) and "held his peace" (Matthew 26:63). What peace was he holding onto? Perhaps the peace and hope that comes from restoration. Notice how Jesus told those that were beating him, "Hereafter shall ye see the Son of man sitting on the right hand of power" (Matthew 26:64). He knew that, although he was suffering a staggering injustice, he shortly would be resurrected to his position of power in the Godhead. Might the law of restoration have influenced—even been the basis for—the perfect virtues of the Redeemer?

In that sense, understanding the law of restoration informs and motivates our living of the gospel. Restoration becomes the soul of the virtue of meekness, the reason to turn the other cheek in temperance. It provides the force behind forgiveness, the right in righteous judgment, and the footsteps in our walk of faith. It is a balm to festering wounds of frustration, the calm in the storm of life. The restoring power of Christ is literally what "restoreth [our] soul" (Psalm 23:3). Without restoration, we daily fret that we won't get what we deserve or retrieve what we have lost. We push and shove. We rant and rage at others. We try forcefully or belligerently to get recompense and restoration on our own. We shout and scream and shake our fists that life isn't fair. Without restoration, meekness and temperance and forgiveness and other Christlike attributes are nearly impossible. With Christ's restoring power, however, everything changes. We find the gift of hope that leads us to abound in good works (see Ether 12:4). Because of the power of restoration, the seeds of Christlike characteristics shoot out their branches within us, allowing us to live under the shade of their blessings of peace.

Receiving Restoration: The Sowing and Growing Seasons

When we learn of the law of restoration we may think, *Yes, yes! I believe all of this! Amen! Hallelujah! Give me back what I've lost! Go ahead, make the wrongs right!* But soon we may also find ourselves thinking, *Why is this taking so long? Why aren't you restoring my blessings* now? *Restoration doesn't work.* Or perhaps, *Am I not doing something I need to be doing to help bring this about?* To make the blessings of Jesus's restoring power available in our lives, it is necessary to understand and live certain fundamental truths related to it. Two of these truths are the *sowing* and the *growing* seasons.

The Sowing Season

One foundational truth is that we must sow now what we desire to reap later. *If we desire to reap God's fruits tomorrow, we can't plant Satan's seeds today.* "Be not deceived," the Apostle Paul said, "God is not mocked: for whatsoever a man soweth, that shall he also reap. . . . [Therefore] let us not be weary in well doing: for in due season we shall reap, if we faint not" (Galatians 6:7, 9). To Buddhists and Hindus this is called *karma.* Christians sometimes call it the "law of the boomerang" or the "law of the harvest," meaning that whatever we send out comes back to us, or that we reap what we sow. Jesus taught, "For with what judgment ye judge, ye shall be judged: and with what measure ye mete, it shall be measured to you again" (Matthew 7:2; see also Luke 6:38). As an example, on several occasions the Savior taught that forgiving others (or not forgiving) has a direct effect on our being forgiven by God (see Matthew 6:12; 18:35; Luke 11:4; D&C 64:9–11). Part of the law of restoration may be stated thus: What we are sending out—or planting—in our lives will return to us, will be restored to us. If

If we trust in Christ's restoring power, then we must strive to live now with an eye toward how we hope to be recompensed later.

we trust in Christ's restoring power, then we must strive to live now with an eye toward how we hope to be recompensed later. Regardless of our circumstances, we should deal out goodness, truth, kindness, and fairness to others, for sowing those good seeds today will enable a future reaping of good fruits.

I have a friend who recently went through a divorce not of his choosing. In spite of his goodness and faithfulness to his wife for over a decade, she wanted something different for her life, turned on him, and was unfaithful. During his deep suffering we spoke often. One difficult day in particular, when he was feeling both depressed and angry, he asked if I could give him a priesthood blessing. As I blessed him, the overwhelming message that came to my mind and heart was the message of restoration: If he would return good for bad, kindness for meanness, love for hate, loyalty for betrayal, he would eventually have good, kindness, love, and loyalty restored to him. I blessed him with those words and felt the Spirit of God testify of their truthfulness. I have no doubt that in the coming years as my friend sends out those virtues they will, one day, be restored to him by Christ. "Love your enemies, bless them that curse you, do good to them that hate you, and pray for them which despitefully use you" (Matthew 5:44), Jesus said in one of his most difficult yet sublime teachings. When things are unjust or unfair or unwarranted, it's easy to descend into personal Mosaic retribution—eyes for eyes, teeth for teeth, hate for hate, and disloyalty for disloyalty. Yet sowing those evil things reaps nothing good in return. We may not be able to control all the events that happen to us—indeed we can't control most of them—but we certainly have the power to plant good seeds regardless of our circumstances, and thus allow Jesus to one day bless us with good in return.

This foundational lesson of the law of restoration's sowing season is summarized perfectly in the Book of Mormon: "The meaning of the word restoration is to bring back again . . . good for that which is good; righteous for that which is righteous; just for that which is just; merciful for that which is merciful. Therefore, my son, see that you are merciful unto your brethren; deal justly, judge righteously, and do good continually; and if ye do all these things then shall ye receive your reward; yea, ye shall have mercy restored unto you again; ye shall have justice restored unto you again; ye shall have a righteous judgment restored unto you again; and ye shall have good rewarded unto you again. For that which ye do send out shall return unto you again, and be restored" (Alma 41:13–15).

The Growing Season

A second foundational truth in the law of restoration is that sowing and reaping are always separated by a growing season. Nothing is ever harvested the same day, neither here in mortality nor spiritually in heaven. The Lord truly will recompense, but—and thanks be to God for this—restoration usually does not happen according to the schedule we desire; it usually requires a space of time. *This is because Jesus's goal isn't just to* give *things to us; it is to* grow *things in us.* There is a reason that God placed "cherubim and a flaming sword" (Moses 4:31) to guard the tree of life after Adam and Eve partook of the forbidden fruit. God wanted Adam and Eve to grow to become more like him. He knew that immediate redemption from their fallen condition would negate the point of their fall in the first place. They needed to work. They needed to bear children. They needed to be justified and sanctified. They needed time to grow.

This space called the growing season gives us opportunities to change and repent. God's mercy is evident in this season because, in light of the law of the harvest, each of us has sown things we don't desire to reap. If the law of restoration took immediate effect, we would be in a world of trouble since we have all, unfortunately, been the one who inflicts the hurt as well as the one who feels the hurt; the one to whom injustice has been dealt and the one doing the dealing. The growing season is a time to realize what we have sown may not be what we want to reap; it provides the "space granted unto man in which he might repent" (Alma 12:24).

A growing season where all things are not immediately restored also enables us to learn patience, humility, and trust in God. Think of what Joseph in Egypt learned as he endured years and years of sowing and growing before finally reaping in return. Unjustly sold as a slave by his own brothers, then falsely accused of rape by Potiphar's wife, Joseph languished in slavery and prison for years. But during this time "the Lord was with Joseph, and shewed him mercy" (Genesis 39:21). God doesn't leave us all alone in the growing season. He strengthens and works with us, giving his grace if we will receive it; in a metaphorical sense sunning, watering, and weeding us. After Joseph endured decades of difficult growing the Lord eventually made up his losses (and then some), restoring him to his family, giving him the wisdom and inspiration to succeed as Pharaoh's chief adviser, and giving him a name that would in time be revered by millions—all things that were originally taken. But perhaps what Joseph reaped most came from his years of learning to trust in God—no matter what—during the season he spent in prison and as a slave. Those years of growing with God helped make Joseph more like Him.

Thus, the growing season changes our perspective of the harvest season. Ironically, because the growing season does what it does to us, often the greater reward isn't what we reap eventually in recompense but what we've become in the process. Understanding the greater benefits and purposes of the growing season helps us move beyond just gritting our teeth and holding on until we are rewarded. Like a student who just stares at the clock until class is over, taking this approach causes us to miss the lessons the Master Teacher intends us to learn. As we wait faithfully upon the restoring Lord, instead of only asking God to make things right, let us also ask him to make things right *in us*. Being open to God's teachings in the growing season allows Christ to work with us, touch us, heal us, strengthen us, and move us beyond the simplicity of "I'm kind to others so that they will be kind to me" to "I'm kind to others because I love God and he has taught me to love his children as he loves me." If we let it, the growing season helps grow Christlike attributes in us such as patience, compassion, long-suffering, gentleness, meekness, and so forth. If we turn to God during the growing season, he will grow us into something more like himself. This season brings out something in us that, had we been immediately restored to our lost or denied blessings, we would never have attained.

A Restitution of All Things

Gratefully, like Job, some of our lost blessings are made up and harvested during this life. "So the Lord blessed the latter end of Job more than his beginning" (Job 42:12). We must understand, however, that the harvest season always comes in God's own way and time (see D&C 88:68), and usually takes place long after the growing season is complete. Much of what Jesus taught about restoration was future restoration. Future bodies. Future heaven. Future recompense. Future relationships. Future blessings.

Through Christ's restoring power, God will ultimately make amends for our mortal wrongs. In light of restoration we must disagree with the lyrics of "Look Down" in the musical *Les Misérables*, when one convict sings: "I've done no wrong! Sweet Jesus, hear my prayer!" and the other prisoners return with, "Look down, look down, Sweet Jesus doesn't care."[11] No, in fact, Jesus *does* care. God has promised that one day all enemies will be subdued under his feet (1 Corinthians 15:25–28), including the enemy of injustice.

There will be recompense and restoration to such an extent that God's children will exclaim: "Great and marvellous are thy works, Lord God Almighty; just and true are thy ways" (Revelation 15:3), so much so that "every nation, kindred, tongue, and people shall see eye to eye and shall confess before God that his judgments are just" (Mosiah 16:1).

Because of Jesus's restoring grace, someday he will make at one all that which is undone. Someday the law of restoration will come not only to the earth on a global scale but to each of us individually. And that restoring knowledge can, and should, give us power in our everyday lives. It should give us hope. It should help us forgive. It should motivate us to live the golden rule. It should inspire us to sow good seeds in today's sowing season and also learn in patience during our growing season. It should give us reason to trust in a God who is fair even when life is unfair. It should help us look in faith through the ashes of our damaged tabernacles to the rebuilt and restored temple inherent within each of us—yes, with a metaphorical angel Moroni on top. Because one day, through the power of Christ, there will be a "restitution of all things" (Acts 3:21).

Further Study Suggestions: The Restoring Power

Study Suggestion 1: The Fall of Adam and Eve

• In order to understand how something is to be restored, it is necessary to understand first what was lost. Study Genesis 1:28–31; Moses 3:8–9; and

Articles of Faith 1:10. What do these verses imply when they state that every-thing grew "abundantly" or "naturally" and that "it was very good" or "par-adisiacal" before the Fall? While doctrinally we believe the Fall was necessary, what may have been unnecessarily lost? What light might this shed on the concept of a complete restoration from the Fall?

Study Suggestion 2: Restoring everything

• Jesus's Atonement rebalances and ultimately restores everything to its divinely intended condition. Study the following examples and notice the power of restoration at work within each: Vicarious work for the dead (1 Corinthians 15:29; 1 Peter 3:18–20; 4:6; D&C 127:5, 8); the Lamanites in the Book of Mormon (Enos 1:13–14); the Jews and the temple in Jerusalem (Isaiah 1:26; Acts 1:6; 2 Nephi 25:11); the latter-day city of Zion in Missouri (D&C 103:11–13); and the Joseph Smith Translation of the Bible (D&C 35:20). These are but a few. As you study the scriptures, what other examples do you find where the power of restoration is at work?

• Recently a man came to me and told me of losing his job unfairly. Instead of sowing anger in return, he sowed patience and forgiveness. Later a better job came his way, recompensing him much more than he had originally lost. How have you seen the Lord's power of restoration at work in your life? Have you written or recorded your experience?

• The power of restoration also encompasses gospel essentials related to marriage, family, and children. *Handbook 2* (2010) says, "Faithful members whose circumstances do not allow them to receive the blessings of eternal marriage and parenthood in this life will receive all promised blessings in the eternities, provided they keep the covenants they have made with God."[12] What experiences have you had with this promised blessing?

Study Suggestion 3: Future restoration

• Much of what Jesus taught implies that full restoration will not take place until his Second Coming. Study the following verses and look for that idea in Jesus's teachings: Matthew 5:4–9; Luke 10:35; 14:12–14.

• For perhaps one of the most beautiful and comforting verses on future restoration, read Revelation 21:4–5.

• Study Acts 3:19–21. What does the phrase "the times of refreshing" mean? Perhaps more importantly, what does the phrase, "Whom the heaven must receive until the times of *restitution of all things*," speaking of Jesus, mean? How is this more than just the restoration of the Church in the latter days?

THE IDENTIFYING POWER OF CHRIST

Although most of us are surrounded by those who know us, we can sometimes feel like no one truly understands us. Who feels what we feel, thinks what we think, and experiences what we experience? Daily we each face challenges, trials, tests, and temptations that no one else—not even a spouse or sibling or dear friend—can perfectly relate with, given our varied backgrounds and situations. In our unique loneliness we wonder, *Who really understands what I am going through? Who can really relate? If no one really knows, who can truly help me?* The answer is Jesus. One of the most comforting powers of Christ centers on the profound truth that our Lord identifies with us because he felt with us. The Savior lovingly condescended to come to earth, live a mortal life (with all its attendant issues), and personally suffer "below them all" (D&C 122:8) for each of us individually. Jesus does not merely sympathetically know of us, but empathetically identifies with us, and thus can intimately comfort and personally guide us. None needs to ever feel alone. There is one who completely understands, empathizes, and knows how to help us. "Who, who can understand? / He, only one" ("Where Can I Turn for Peace?" *Hymns*, no. 129).

Chapter 4

THE IDENTIFYING POWER OF CHRIST

In all their afflictions he was afflicted.

—Doctrine and Covenants 133:53

Sometimes when I teach about Jesus suffering for us, I will have my students close their eyes while I place a rock in their hand. With their eyes still closed, I tell them they have one minute to get to know their rock by touch only—not by sight. They feel their rock's corners, crags, and crevices, assessing its weight in their hands and features on their fingertips. Then, with their eyes still closed, they place the rock back into a large sack, where it becomes lost among dozens of other unique and varied rocks that have been handled by other students. When I tell them to open their eyes and find their rock, they do so energetically, picking up various stones to closely feel them, putting back stone after stone until someone triumphantly claims, "This is my rock!"

"How do you know it's your rock?" I ask, "How did you recognize it?"

"Because it has this lump here," or "It's got this crack there," they say. They can identify their rock because they have intimately felt it.

71

Similarly, one of the divine powers of Christ centers on the profound truth that our Savior identifies with us because he intimately felt *with* us. Astoundingly, we worship a God who had the power to create and govern a world and then voluntarily chose to live upon it together with all his other creations. The mighty premortal Jehovah of Creation became the mortal Babe of Bethlehem and a common carpenter from Nazareth. "The Word was made flesh, and dwelt among us" (John 1:14), John the Beloved wrote, which verse in Greek, literally translated, means that Jesus "pitched his tent among us"—becoming one of our fellow campers.[1] Why did he choose to do this? Why did the Creator become mortal? "Well, to overcome death for us," one might say. "To suffer for our sins," another believer may answer. True and true. However, did Jehovah have to come here as an *infant*, to be born and raised and then crucified at thirty-three? Could he not have made a briefer appearance, riding off of premortal clouds straight into his triumphal entry in Jerusalem? Why did he have to live a complete mortal life?

> Our Savior identifies with us because he intimately felt with us.

The reasons go back to the rocks: To save us from all that mortality encompasses, Christ had to experience it to truly identify with us. His complete mortal life was a necessary part of his saving qualifications. In this sense, the Atonement did not occur over one weekend. It took place each day of the Lord's life, from birth to death, as he experienced and successfully overcame all aspects of mortality. "And he shall go forth," Alma taught—which phrase implies Jesus's *daily* experience in the flesh and not just an end-of-life event—"suffering pains and afflictions and temptations" (Alma 7:11). Jesus's day-to-day challenges allow him to understand and help us in our day-to-day challenges. Jesus lived a mortal life to become a perfectly empathetic Savior capable of guiding us to eternal lives (*see Study Suggestion 1*). What follows in this chapter is how Jesus did it, why he did it, and what it should mean for us in our efforts to receive of his divine power in our day-to-day lives.

> The Atonement did not occur over one weekend. It took place each day of the Lord's life, from birth to death, as he experienced and successfully overcame all aspects of mortality.

Ascension through Condescension

The Book of Mormon introduces us to a wonderful term, the condescension of Christ (2 Nephi 4:26). *Condescend* means to come down from a high station to a low station, or "to descend to a less formal or dignified level"; "to waive the privileges of rank."[2] Condescension in a worldly sense would be like LeBron James retiring from the NBA in his prime to play as a reserve on your elders quorum basketball team, or Celine Dion happily singing harmony in your fledgling ward choir, or Microsoft founder Bill Gates giving away all his money to take a graveyard shift at a factory. In heavenly terms, condescension is God agreeing to leave his exalted station in heaven, waiving his privileges as a member of the Godhead, and descending to the lowliest of stations on earth—born as a help-less baby in a dirty cave in a backward town to an impoverished and obscure family in a politically oppressed nation. The God who formed worlds without number (see Moses 1:33) and had the very elements obey his voice (see Abraham 4; Helaman 12:8) became a helpless infant who couldn't speak, becoming completely depen-dent upon the very flesh he would redeem, being cared for by first-time parents with pure hearts but inexperienced hands. *God became a mortal, like you and me, in every sense of the word.*

Jesus's Humanity

From the moment Jesus was born to Mary and wrapped his celestial spirit in telestial flesh he became like us in his mortality. In spite of the sentimental Christmas hymn "Away in a Manger," as a baby little Lord Jesus probably cried a lot. Most babies do. Presumably he fussed and didn't sleep through the night. He probably tried to put everything in his mouth. He rolled over, and then crawled, and then stumbled to an unsteady walk. He possibly threw temper tantrums and cried until he fell asleep on the floor, cheeks flushed and hair tousled with sweat. He babbled and had to learn how to make word associations.

Ironically, he who made the trees had to learn how to say "tree." I once held my two-year-old son Calvin in my arms and pointed to a tree, and he responded with, "Dog."

"No," I said, "that's a tree, buddy. Can you say *tree?*"

"Tuh-ree," he syllabled out proudly. I imagine Joseph holding two-year-old Jesus and having the same conversation: "Can you say tree, Jesus? Good! Let's go show your mom. Mary! He knows how to say *tree*!"

Like all of us, our Lord experienced the veil of forgetfulness.[3] Jesus had to learn he was Jehovah. When did he realize he was special, was the Messiah? We don't really know. It is evident by the time he was twelve years old in the temple that he already understood who his real Father was and that his life's purpose was to do God's will (see Luke 2:49). Despite this knowledge, however, Jesus continued to develop as a regular boy. He probably preferred to play and run with his friends instead of doing chores around the house. Like many boys, he may have loved being outside and enjoyed the beauties of nature. He likely ran foot races, and probably lost as often as he won. His mind was brilliant, for sure, but perhaps he forgot things—misplaced his father's tools, lost track of the time, had to be reminded of something. The story when he was twelve at the temple is evidence of that, as he overlooked telling his parents where he was, causing an unnecessary three-day search for a missing boy. There's no sin in any of this. It was just part of his physical, mental, social, and spiritual development, which Jesus had to experience as he grew into a man (see Luke 2:52). None of what I have written here implies any impropriety in God's Divine Son. It implies mortality. It reminds us of the condescension of the Son of God (*see Study Suggestion 2*).

Jesus's Temptations and Mistakes

Jesus not only experienced mortal life as we do but also experienced temptation as we do, in all its difficulty. *The Lord felt the tugs of temptation on his divine robe and had to reject its pulls, just like the rest of us*. He had to resist feelings of pride and selfishness—the most common of all human vices. Jesus faced usual temptations of dishonesty, deceit, laziness, lust, anger, overindulgence, and the like. You name your temptations with sin, and Jesus felt them too. We are wrong when we think that Jesus was only grandly tempted of the devil on one occasion, sometimes called the "temptations of Jesus" (see Matthew 4:1–11), which is a misnomer. Luke adds the important detail that the devil departed Jesus "for a season" (Luke 4:13) after this experience. In reality his varied temptations continued day after day during his mortal life and ministry (see Luke 22:28), although he marvelously "gave no heed unto them" (D&C 20:22). Speaking of this familiarity with temptation, the Apostle Paul tells us, "For we have not an high priest [Jesus] which cannot be touched with the feeling of our infirmities; but was in all points tempted like as we are, yet without sin" (Hebrews 4:15). Speaking from empathy and not sympathy, the Lord said in the Doctrine and Covenants that he is "Jesus Christ, your advocate, *who knoweth the weakness of man* and how to succor them who are tempted" (D&C 62:1; emphasis added). The New Testament says, "The Lord knoweth how to deliver the godly out of temptations" (2 Peter 2:9). Why? Because he experienced and resisted temptations in his life as well.

While unequivocally stating that Jesus never wrestled with his temptations nor rebelled or sinned, I equally believe that Jesus's perfect sinlessness doesn't mean he never made any mistakes. There is a difference between sin and error (see D&C 1:25, 27).[4] The joints on Jesus's carpentry corners may not have been perfectly square at first, literally or metaphorically. *The Savior had to learn line upon line like us all, which implies at certain points he may not have known all the lines he should follow.* Where there is no law, there is no sin (see Romans 4:15; 2 Nephi 9:25), even for Jesus. The Doctrine and Covenants provides us with profound insight on this concept, telling us that Jesus "received not of the fulness at the first, but received grace for grace; and he received not of the fulness at first, but continued from grace to grace, until he received a fulness" (D&C 93:12–13). These are fascinating verses that imply that Jesus did not have a fulness of knowledge, power, intelligence, light, and truth throughout his whole life. They built and peaked at the end of his mortal life. He gradually grew into them, including gradually grasping a perfect knowledge of exactly what he should and shouldn't do.

When I was a boy, my best friend, David, and I stripped all the bark off of a tree in my home's backyard because we liked how smooth the raw wood was underneath the bark. We spent hours happily stripping the tree of its seemingly unnecessary outer skin. It wasn't until we showed my parents our wondrous work and saw the looks on their faces that we realized we had done something wrong—something that ended up killing the tree. We simply hadn't understood. Similarly, Jesus may have made mistakes he didn't realize were wrong until he was later taught, line upon line. Indeed, the Savior "*learned* . . . obedience by the things which he suffered" (Hebrews 5:8; emphasis added). As Jesus learned he always perfectly obeyed, and thus through his perfect obedience exponentially grew in more light and truth (see D&C 93:28, 39) until he eventually received a fulness of light, truth, understanding, intelligence, glory, and power after his resurrection (see Matthew 28:18). As on the rungs of a ladder, Jesus climbed from level to level, obedience by obedience, step by step, or from "grace to grace, until he received a fulness" (D&C 93:13). Jesus personally understands temptations as well as mistakes, learning, growth, and progression.

This mortal reality of Jesus doesn't demean him, it deifies him. Abinadi teaches us that "because of the flesh" Jesus was enabled to be a God (Mosiah 15:3), a teaching so profound in its theological implications that the idea led to Abinadi's death (see Mosiah 17:7–8). In a life of difficulty, however, how could we really worship a God who was exempt? How could we seek deliverance from temptation and look to someone as an exemplar who has never resisted it himself? How could we turn to a God to help us grow and change who hadn't learned to grow and change too? *How is it possible to ask a God to dry tears that he himself has never shed? (see Study Suggestion 3).*

> Jesus personally understands temptations as well as mistakes, learning, growth, and progression.

Jesus's humanity comprises an essential aspect of his divinity. Much of our divine worship of him is centered on his mortal suffering with us. "Wherefore in all things it behoved him to be made like unto his brethren, that he might be a merciful and faithful high priest" (Hebrews 2:17). In a beautiful illustration of this idea, the Free Church minister and poet Edward Shillito wrote, in "Jesus of the Scars":

> *The other gods were strong, but Thou wast weak;*
> *They rode, but Thou didst stumble to a throne*

But to our wounds only God's wounds can speak,
And not a god has wounds, but Thou alone.[5]

Jesus's empathy, however, extends beyond the experience and suffering of a normal human being—even beyond that of any mortal. What is it that enabled him to identify with *everyone* as Savior, and not just Jewish males in the meridian of time? The scriptures teach us that Jesus (1) descended *below* all things, that (2) he might ascend *above* all things (see D&C 88:6). Understanding each of these truths is key to unlocking the divine identifying power of Christ in our individual and varied daily lives.

Christ Descended below All Things

When Jesus crossed the brook Cedron and entered the Garden of Gethsemane late that fateful Passover night, he crossed a threshold beyond any human experience, into something only he could endure and none of us could imagine. Within the next twenty-four hours he would experience "even more than man can suffer" (Mosiah 3:7)—the consequences of sin, the fierce demands and wrath of justice, and the all-out hell that Lucifer and his unholy demonic legions mustered to try and thwart the Redeemer. It is beyond the scope of this chapter to expound upon that portion of atoning theology which entails how and why Jesus satisfied justice's demands through his suffering for humanity's sins.[6] More germane to the identifying power of Christ is an additional part of his atoning suffering—a part which wasn't perhaps necessary to satisfy the demands of justice and redeem men from their fallen, sinful state: Jesus's suffering for all aspects of our mortality.

In what Elder Neal A. Maxwell eloquently called the "awful arithmetic of the Atonement,"[7] Jesus not only expiated the sins of humanity, but somehow also suffered the pains, sicknesses, and infirmities of all mankind who had ever lived or would yet live. The Book of Mormon prophet Jacob said that Jesus would experience "the pains of every living creature, both men, women, and children, who belong to the family of Adam" (2 Nephi 9:21). Alma taught that Christ would not only "take upon him the pains" of his people, but also "the sicknesses of his people" and "their infirmities" (Alma 7:11–12). Given the incalculable breadth and depth of human emotion, pain, and suffering, these are pits of personal hell through which Jesus passed that we cannot possibly fathom. It is suffering so intense that in the only firsthand account given by Jesus of his atoning anguish, the Savior doesn't even finish the sentence: "Which suffering caused myself, even God, the greatest of all, to tremble because of pain, and to bleed at every pore, and to suffer both body and spirit—and would that I might not drink the bitter cup, and shrink—" (D&C 19:18). The Savior leaves off telling us about a suffering we mortals couldn't comprehend even if the Son of God had explained it. All we know for certain from the scriptural record is that "the Son of Man hath descended below them all" (D&C 122:8). He suffered further than any other mortal ever has, will—or can.

Jesus's suffering was not only vastly deep, but extremely personal. Elder Merrill J. Bateman described this empathetic aspect of Jesus's suffering as "intimate as well as infinite,"[8] giving his personal perspective that in the Garden of Gethsemane and on the cross Jesus saw each of us and experienced our deepest feelings.[9]

We don't know how this divine act of infinite, individualized suffering came about, and there needs to be caution here on this point. Did Jesus *literally* experience all the happenings of humanity on that night? When speaking with Robert L. Millet, former dean of Religious Education at BYU, on this subject, he said to me, "Did Jesus really suffer delivery pains in Gethsemane? Did he suffer an ACL tear? Did he receive a rejection letter from Stanford? Or, rather, is it the case that his perfect empathy comes out of his perfect love?" That is a great question.

Here's a case in point: When my son Eli was three years old he tried to hop up on our kitchen countertop and slipped, his eye catching the full force of the fall, splitting his brow wide open. I quickly took him to the urgent care clinic to be treated, leaving a message for my wife about what had happened. While the doctor began to treat the gash on my little boy I stood next to him holding his hand. I normally am not one to be woozy or bothered at the sight of blood or injuries, but when the doctor began cleansing my son's wound I suddenly felt my legs go limp and my head get light. I literally felt a hurt inside my heart, feeling pain *with* my son. Although I didn't have my eye split open, in some way I was experiencing it too. My deep love for my boy caused me deep feelings of pain, so much so that I had to sit down. It may be that Jesus's personal suffering for us individually was more like that—feeling our individual pain through the connective tissue of love without literally experiencing it. Only heaven knows how it happened.

Whatever the answer may be, the gospel reality is that a connection was made that night through the Lord's infinite suffering to each of us who suffer. Elder David A. Bednar taught: "There is no physical pain, no spiritual wound, no anguish of soul or heart-ache, no infirmity or weakness you or I ever confront in mortality that the Savior did not experience first. In a moment of weakness we may cry out, 'No one knows what it is like. No one understands.' But the Son of God perfectly knows and understands, for He has felt and borne our individual burdens."[10]

Perhaps this is why Isaiah taught that "in all [our] affliction [Jesus] was afflicted" (Isaiah 63:9). Somehow Jesus of Nazareth felt and suffered with Anthony Sweat from Utah and equally for each of the billions of God's children globally—past, present, and future. This theological reality gives additional meaning to the scripture "Inasmuch as ye have done it unto one of the least of these my brethren, ye have done it unto me" (Matthew 25:40). Suffering so personally like this may seem impossible, yet with God, we know that all things are possible (Luke 1:37). Somehow through his infinite atoning sacrifice, Jesus gained perfect empathy for each of us individually.

Christ Is above All Things

Because Jesus suffered in all things for all people, "*he comprehendeth all things*, and all things are before him, and all things are round about him; *and he is above all things*" (D&C 88:41; emphasis added). We sing, "Jesus, Savior, pilot me / Over life's tempestuous sea"[11] because he has already successfully sailed all the waters of mortality. None of us is ever completely on our own, and nobody needs to go it alone. While each of us is in a unique situation and at times misunderstood by others, nobody can accurately or rightly say to heaven, "You don't understand," because our Savior does. "We can confidently cast our cares upon the Lord," said Elder Neal A. Maxwell, because "through the agonizing events of Gethsemane and Calvary, atoning Jesus is already familiar with our sins, sicknesses, and sorrows. He can carry them now because He has successfully carried them before."[12]

The scriptures are clear that Jesus suffered for all of us so he can empathetically guide us. *Succor* is the word often used, meaning "to give assistance or aid." After articulating the range of Jesus's mortal and atoning suffering, Alma says that he did all of this "that his bowels may be filled with mercy, according to the flesh, that he may know according to the flesh how to succor his people according to their infirmities" (Alma 7:12). Paul says, "For in that he himself hath suffered being tempted, he is able to succour them that are tempted" (Hebrews 2:18).

Thus, because Jesus has successfully suffered and overcome *all* things, he can help us in *our* things. That is why his day-to-day mortal experience became a necessary part of his day-to-day saving divinity; it makes the Lord our ultimate counselor. We gain our greatest support from networks of those who have experienced what we are experiencing. We don't typically turn to our single twenty-two-year-old neighbor for quality teenage parenting direction. We turn to other parents who have previous experience with or who are currently successfully parenting teenagers. There is a reason a doctoral dissertation committee is comprised of PhDs, and it's not

Because Jesus has successfully suffered and overcome all things, he can help us in our things.

just to intimidate the doctoral candidate—they've been there, done that, and know how to help others through the experience. Christ's identifying power supersedes them all in perfect support and help because of his infinite experience. *Christ's mortal condescension enables our eternal ascension.*

Counseling with the Man of Counsel

To those who feel alone, Jesus's identifying power says you are never alone, promising that "I will not leave you comfortless: I will come to you" (John 14:18). This empathetic promise applies to the first-time mother, the grieving widower, the new kid at school, the prisoner, the homeless, the addict, the dying. It also applies to any who feel that no one understands, yet wish someone who could help them would. Because of his perfect empathy for what we are currently going through, Christ always stands by us, "on your right hand and on your left, and my Spirit [is] in your hearts . . . to bear you up" (D&C 84:88).

I've come to believe that the reason that those who trust in Christ can "mourn with those that mourn; yea, and comfort those that stand in need of comfort, and to stand as witnesses of God at all times and in all things, and in all places that ye may be in" (Mosiah 18:9) is that Jesus first does all that to them. "We love him," the Apostle John wrote, "because he first loved us" (1 John 4:19). To find daily power in Christ, however, it isn't enough just to know that Jesus descended below all things for us and that through his identifying love he suffers together with us. Remember, he suffered below all things so that he could rise above all things—for us. *Thus, a direct, daily application of the identifying power is to listen to the counsel that comes to us through the Lord's Spirit as we seek divine direction in our daily lives.* "Learn of me, and listen to my words; walk in the meekness of my Spirit, and you shall have peace in me" (D&C 19:23), the Lord tells us. Like a coach who can see the field of life from an infinite number of high-definition camera angles, Christ calls perfect, individualized plays for our benefit and the benefit of others.

Whatever it is we are facing today, we can turn to Christ and say, "How should I handle this? What should I do?" and he can in turn say, "I understand. I have walked this mortal path. Let me teach you from my experience. Let me show you the way. Let me show you how to faithfully overcome this." Speaking of why you should turn to the Savior "for your deliverance and comfort," Elder Jeffrey R. Holland said it is because "the Savior has been where you have been."[13] Elder Neal A. Maxwell taught that it is because of Jesus's perfect "empathy and His mercy" that he has perfect "capacity to succor us, for which we can be everlastingly grateful as He tutors us in our trials."[14]

Thus, the divine command to "counsel with the Lord in all thy doings" (Alma 37:37) stems from not only God's omnipotence (all power) and omniscience (all knowledge), but his omnipassion (all suffering) as well. A direct, daily application of this identifying truth is for us "to look unto [Christ] in every thought" and thus to "doubt not, fear not" (D&C 6:36). It is for us to "pour out [our] souls in [our] closets, and [our] secret places" (Alma 34:26) and empty everything on the table in prayer to God—to speak to him our innermost thoughts and feelings and worries and questions and concerns—

I'm struggling with . . .

I'm worried about . . .

I don't know what to do about . . .

Help me understand why . . .

How did you deal with . . .

What would you have me to do about . . .

—and then listen, feel, and learn. In turn, Christ, through the Spirit, may convey feelings to you, something along the lines of

"I know what you're going through . . ."

"I feel your pain with you . . ."

"Let me teach you how to respond to that . . ."

"Let me show you the way to go . . ."

"I know what that's like; let me tell you what to do . . ."

"The best way you should handle this right now is to . . ."

Thus, we are told to "trust in the Lord with all thine heart; and lean not unto thine own understanding. In all thy ways acknowledge him, and he shall direct thy paths" (Proverbs 3:5–6). Our receiving of this everyday identifying power comes from our counseling with the Man of Counsel, and then listening to the directions that come from God's Spirit. Understanding this identifying truth helps us to receive the comfort, direction, guidance, and perfect empathy from Jesus that we need to face and overcome our day-to-day challenges. Jesus can perfectly guide us today because he perfectly identifies with us, always.

You Are Not Alone

If we exercise faith in him, each of us may have the profound knowledge that our Savior perfectly knows us, loves us, understands us, and is with us in our day-to-day lives. As he promises us in the Doctrine and Covenants, "I will go before your face. I will be on your right hand and on your left, and my Spirit shall be in your hearts, and mine angels round about you, to bear you up" (D&C 84:88). He can bear us up now because he bore all things before. "Surely he hath borne *our* griefs, and carried *our* sorrows" Isaiah reassured (Isaiah 53:4; emphasis added). None of us need think we are ever alone or forgotten or that no one understands us. None of us needs to be at a loss for what to do. This very day, this very hour, our Lord identifies with our unique personal situations, challenges, temptations, and struggles. "Thy walls [our challenges] are continually before me," he reminds us. "I have graven thee upon the palms of my hands" (Isaiah 49:16). Let us turn to him today for his divine counsel and guidance and find hope in his complete understanding of and answers for our mortal problems. He will not forsake us nor abandon us. He will not leave us alone. He will not leave us comfortless. He will come to us and succor us. He is Jesus the Christ, with divine power to identify with and guide us in all times and in all things and in all places that we may be in.

Further Study Suggestions: The Identifying Power

Study Suggestion 1: Empathy, not sympathy

• There is a major difference between sympathy and empathy. Sympathy means that we "feel for" someone, like when we hear a news story in a distant place and our hearts go out to those affected by disaster or innocently suffering. Empathy, on the other hand, means to "feel into," or to understand another's suffering because we have suffered or experienced it ourselves. Although often a natural human emotion, why can sympathy sometime create distance? How does empathy close distance? What does this concept have to do with Jesus—and us? Why might a God of sympathy be insufficient?

• The word *compassion* is derived from *empathy*, literally meaning to suffer with someone (*com* = "with" and *passion* = "suffering"). Study the following verses that illustrate Christ's empathetic compassion: Matthew 9:36; 14:14; 15:32; 20:34; Mark 1:41; 9:22; Luke 7:13. What other scriptural verses can you find that illustrate Christ's suffering with us?

Study Suggestion 2: Jesus's humanity

• Picture Jesus as a seventeen-year-old boy. How does he look? What does he act like? In what ways is he a normal teenager, yet still God's divine son? Picture him getting up in the morning; doing chores; being instructed, directed, and even corrected by his earthly parents, Mary and Joseph. What does he understand and what does he not? How did he learn who he was, what his divine earthly mission was? Was it different from how we learn who we are and our mission? If yes, how? If not, then what does that teach you?

• Study D&C 93:1–40. This is a profound revelation teaching us "how to worship" and "what you worship" (highlight that thesis statement in D&C 93:17). What do you learn about how and what to worship from these verses?

• Study D&C 93:6–16. These ten verses are apparently the writings of John the Baptist. Consider the following:

(1) In verse 11, John transitions with wonder to Jesus's mortal condescension. Read verses 12–14 and highlight that John emphasizes three times that Jesus "received not a fulness at first." Why does he repeatedly say this?

What does it mean that he didn't receive a fulness at first? At the first of what? A fulness of what? Search D&C 93 and other verses (such as Matthew 28:18) for potential insights. How did Jesus gain a fulness? See D&C 93:12–13. What does "grace *for* grace" (v. 12) mean? Is it different from "grace *to* grace"? (v. 13). Read D&C 93:20, 26–28 for potential insights.

(2) Read D&C 93:20. What may God intend for you to learn about yourself from this verse and the concept of grace for grace?

• Read Elder Dallin H. Oaks's talk "Sins and Mistakes" (*Ensign*, October 1996, 62–67). What might this concept teach us about Jesus's perfection?

Study Suggestion 3: Jesus's human feelings and emotions

• Although sometimes portrayed as consistently stoic in some media, the scriptures suggest Christ experienced a range of human feelings and emotions. Read the following verses that suggest just some of these: Thirst (John 4:7; 19:28), hunger (Matthew 21:18), and fatigue (Matthew 8:25; John 4:6). Frustration "with anger" (Mark 3:5) and "zeal" (John 2:17) to the point of being consumed. Sorrow and sadness (Mark 10:14), being "troubled" in spirit (John 11:33; 13:21), depressing thoughts to the point of death (Matthew 26:38; Mark 14:34). Love (John 13:1), fear (Luke 22:42), and joy (John 15:11). Sadness for the choices of others (Luke 19:41) and for the death of loved ones (John 11:34–36). Search the scriptures and find other feelings and emotions Jesus exhibited that are not mentioned herein. What do you find? More importantly, what do you learn?

• Jesus knows the longing of loneliness. Study the following passages that suggest that feelings of isolation, abandonment, and loneliness were required parts of the Savior's testing and mission: Matthew 27:46; John 16:32; D&C 76:107; 122:8; 133:50. Why is suffering alone prevalent in the Savior's mission?

THE STRENGTHENING POWER OF CHRIST

Who of us doesn't stand in need of divine strength and help today? Who can mentally review their individual list of tasks and challenges and then look him- or herself in the mirror and honestly say, "I've got this . . ." without truly seeing that the only thing he or she has "got" is probably more than they can handle on their own? Each of us has daily burdens to bear, temptations to resist, and difficult work that demands our best. God promises us that he is not only aware of our unique challenges but that, if we will depend on him, he will also divinely strengthen us to successfully meet and overcome those challenges. Through the "strength of the Lord," we are promised at least three types of daily help: (1) Help to successfully bear our burdens and trials; (2) Help to resist temptation and overcome sin; and (3) Help to do good works beyond our natural capacity. Our daily question toward the heavens is often, "Will you help me?" and the astounding answer from Christ in return is, "I'll strengthen thee, help thee, and cause thee to stand, / . . . Upheld by my righteous, omnipotent hand" ("How Firm a Foundation," *Hymns*, no. 85).

Chapter 5

THE STRENGTHENING POWER OF CHRIST

Hast thou not known? hast thou not heard, that the
everlasting God . . . giveth power to the faint; and
to them that have no might he increaseth strength.

—Isaiah 40:28–29

Although I enjoy watching *The New Yankee Workshop* and doing *This Old House* building projects, if the Lord asked me to hand-build a ship to carry my family, parents, siblings, and some neighbors across an ocean, I would have some serious reservations—as would my loved ones, and rightly so. Why then did Nephi act with such assurance when the Lord commanded him, "Thou shalt construct a ship" (1 Nephi 17:8) to carry the families of Lehi and Ishmael across an ocean? Not only was Nephi denied the blessings of modern PBS woodworking shows and YouTube tutorials, it's doubtful that he or his family had any real experience with shipmaking before arriving at the sea of Irreantum (see 1 Nephi 17:17–19). However, Nephi didn't question whether he could build the ship, but instead offered a simple, astoundingly faithful question to God in return, "Whither shall I go that I may find ore to molten, that I may make tools to construct the ship?" (1 Nephi 17:9). Remarkably, Nephi's only reported concern was where to find the materials, not if he could do the task. *That would be akin to someone who had never touched a piano being called to play the organ for the Mormon Tabernacle Choir and simply answering, "Whither shall I go that I might obtain soft pedal shoes wherewith to play?"* Where did Nephi get this assurance—that his brothers would shortly mock as absurd—and how can we have the same confidence to face the seemingly impossible challenges that confront us in our lives? To answer that question we need to back up a few pages in the Book of Mormon and look at Nephi's previous experiences, experiences which built the hull of the ship of faith that he so confidently sailed throughout his prophetic life—a faith fortified by the power of Christ's grace.

Nephi's Thesis: God Will Make Us Mighty

Like a good writer, Nephi provides a thesis statement in his introductory chapter of 1 Nephi: "I, Nephi, will show unto you that the tender mercies of the Lord are over all those whom he hath chosen, because of their faith, *to make them mighty even unto the power of deliverance*" (1 Nephi 1:20; emphasis added). His general theme is not just obedience to God, but what obedience provides us: divine power to overcome obstacles. In the subsequent chapters of his first book, Nephi provides no less than five examples—fleeing from Jerusalem, obtaining the brass plates, God freeing him from his brothers' murderous plot, successes and failures with the Liahona, and the women being made strong like unto the men—to illustrate and support his thesis that God gives divine strength and enabling power to the faithful to overcome difficulties (*see Study Suggestion 1*).

After recounting these five major events, Nephi concludes: "And thus we see that the commandments of God must be fulfilled.

And if it so be that the children of men keep the commandments of God *he doth nourish them, and strengthen them, and provide means* whereby they can accomplish the thing which he has commanded them" (1 Nephi 17:3; emphasis added). Is it any wonder, then, that after these varied experiences, when the Lord asked Nephi to build a ship, Nephi so confidently accepted the challenge? Nephi had learned of, accessed, and experienced the strengthening power of Christ—the divine power that enables us to do things beyond our natural capacity—and thus was able to boldly bear the burdens, trials, and temptations with which he would be faced throughout the remainder of his life. Like Nephi, if we are to face and overcome our modern tests in their varied and distinct forms, we must daily tap into and receive this same enabling, strengthening grace from our Lord, Jesus Christ.

Scriptural Examples of Divine Strength

The concept that the Lord can give us divine strength beyond our natural ability is not just a major theme of Nephi's writings, but in *all* of scripture. Think of the Old Testament stories: Moses performs divine miracles to free Israel from bondage; Joshua brings down walls and conquers the promised land; Gideon delivers; David crushes Goliath; Solomon is given divine wisdom above all other men; Elijah seals the heavens, multiplies food, and calls down fire, and his near-namesake Elisha does the same; Esther is given courage to save the Jews; Daniel interprets dreams and shuts lions' mouths; temples are rebuilt, walls are put up, and miracle after miracle is accomplished by those who are strengthened and given divine help by God.

The New Testament is no different: A young woman becomes the mother of the Savior; a common man named Peter uncommonly walks on the very water he fished upon; and speaking of fish—a boy's five fishes are multiplied by the Lord to feed five thousand.

In the Book of Mormon, anti-Christs are confounded; converts are gained as arms are lost; prison walls tumble to the earth; secret combinations are destroyed; sacred records are made and preserved.

And in our own day, this dispensation begins with the marvelous work and wonder of an unlearned farm boy—one who couldn't "write nor dictate a coherent and well-worded letter," according to his wife[1]—given power to look into seer stones and translate the Book of Mormon in all its literary complexity and spiritual profundity. Amazing. Just as the Lord's grace is infinite, so too are the names of everyday people across all ages, times, backgrounds, and circumstances who have been divinely helped and strengthened by Christ—including today.

An Everyday Power for the Everyday Person

While *grace* can have many definitions,[2] I believe the simplest way to describe it is "loving help from God." The following summary in the Bible Dictionary has perhaps become best known within a Mormon context: "The main idea of the word [grace] is divine means of help or strength, given through the bounteous mercy and love of Jesus Christ. . . . This grace is an enabling power."[3] Elder David A. Bednar has spoken often in his ministry of the helping or strengthening quality of Christ's atoning grace.[4] In his first address as a newly called member of the Quorum of the

Twelve Apostles, he said, "The enabling and strengthening aspect of the Atonement helps us to see and to do and to become good in ways that we could never recognize or accomplish with our limited mortal capacity."[5] The Apostle Paul was the New Testament version of Elder Bednar in this respect, speaking often of the Lord's grace and strengthening power: "And he said unto me, My grace is sufficient for thee: for my strength is made perfect in weakness. Most gladly therefore will I rather glory in my infirmities, that the power of Christ may rest upon me" (2 Corinthians 12:9). And Paul's famous one-line summary: "I can do all things through Christ which strengtheneth me" (Philippians 4:13).

The Book of Mormon repeatedly speaks of the "strength of the Lord" (see 1 Nephi 4:31; Words of Mormon 1:14; Alma 46:20). Often that phrase is used in connection with battle (see Alma 61:18; 3 Nephi 4:10; Mormon 2:26). My favorite use of the phrase comes from Ammon who, after his miraculous years of missionary service to the Lamanites, said: "I will boast of my God, for in his strength I can do all things" (Alma 26:12). Those last eight words echoed in my mind and heart to such a degree at a time when I daily doubted my ability to meet the challenges pressing upon me that I typed the phrase *In his strength I can do all things* on the top of my schedule of deadlines to remind me daily that with God's help I could indeed accomplish all the work that I felt divinely driven to do. The scriptures taught me that if Jesus had strengthened Paul, Ammon, Elder Bednar, and others, he could also strengthen me in my labors.

Like God's divine love, the Lord's divine strength is offered to all, Jew and Gentile, young and old, bond and free, male and female. The strengthening power of Christ is available to the everyday person—every day. It is not a gift that is unique to prophets and prophetesses. It is not confined to a specific calling, geographic location, time, beard length, or bonnet. *The modern mother can be as enabled as the past prophet. The father of four strengthened just as was faithful Father Abraham.* A young mother recently shared the following experience with me about how the grace of Christ strengthened her in everyday life—in this case, helping in a time of frustration and exhaustion:

"One night for some reason my newborn baby was so restless. Every time I tried to lay her down she would start wailing—not just crying—so I'd have to hold her. As the clock grew closer to 2:00 or 3:00 A.M. and my arms ached and my whole body felt exhausted, I grew frustrated and angry with my daughter. It had been hours of soothing and pacing the floor of my room at this point. It was her fault that I would be exhausted the next day and therefore have no patience with my other children. I began to feel resentful and agitated. Suddenly I had an idea to pick up my iPad and listen to the church hymns I had on it. So that is what I did. I searched for ones that pertained to my situation and there

The strengthening power of Christ is available to the everyday person— every day.

were two that provided the solace I needed: 'Abide with Me, 'Tis Eventide' and 'I Need Thee Every Hour.' I truly felt like I needed Him *every* hour at this point because I couldn't take it anymore. Although my baby didn't stop crying and I ended up staying up almost all night with her, I felt like God was speaking to me—like He understood me and that I wasn't alone and that strengthened me. I was reminded by God that my children aren't just mine—they are my responsibility in this mortal life—but that our Father is their Father. I used to think the Lord's Atonement was only for repentance, but I've learned that His Atonement is here for our mortal journey to give us strength beyond our capability."

While our daily challenges may vary in type, intensity, and frequency, there seem to be three general areas in which we can seek and receive divine help in our lives: (1) Strength to faithfully endure trials and challenges; (2) Strength to overcome sin and temptation; and (3) Strength to perform work beyond our own natural capacities. The strengthening power of Christ is designed and available for all three of these types of daily tests.

Strength to Meet Trials and Challenges

Although often unspoken or unknown to others, daily burdens are borne by all people. "In the quiet heart is hidden / Sorrow that the eye can't see"[6] isn't just beautiful poetry, it's painfully accurate too. Some face daily challenges related to work and finances, while others need help in their marriages and families. Some are tested daily through a physical disability or persistent pain. Within a regular day's work I noted multiple examples of trial and difficulty: a student with a severe speech impediment, another who could not attend class because of unexpected illness, a colleague who felt unfairly treated, a young woman who had fallen behind in her coursework because of trauma related to an assault, and overwhelming grief of friends of a student tragically killed in an accident.

While we are sure to experience difficulty in life, one of the promises in scripture is that, regardless of the source of our trial, Christ can give us strength to meet and successfully bear our burdens. "How long shall we suffer these great afflictions, O Lord? O Lord, give us strength according to our faith which is in Christ, even unto deliverance" (Alma 14:26) was the plea of Alma and Amulek when they were unjustly imprisoned, and God gave them strength and deliverance. "He giveth power to the faint; and to them that have no might he increaseth strength," said Isaiah. "Even the youths shall faint and be weary, and the young men shall utterly fall: But they that wait upon the Lord shall renew their strength; they shall mount up with wings as eagles; they shall run, and not be weary; and they shall walk, and not faint" (Isaiah 40:29–31). Like Shadrach, Meshach, and Abed-nego, the Lord can give us divine courage and protection to conquer our obstacles in our fiery furnace of affliction. Like Ruth and Naomi, the Lord can grant us courage, faith, wisdom, and solutions to overcome our challenges and difficulties. Or like Amanda Smith—who miraculously healed the hip of her son who was wounded during the Haun's Mill massacre[7]—the Lord can inspire our minds with instructions and answers to solve problems when we don't know what to do.

Sometimes, though, the burden or trial isn't removed for a long time, if at all, such as in the case of a permanent disability or familial disintegration. What then? The Book of Mormon teaches us that sometimes God doesn't eradicate the burden, but he gives us spiritual strength to carry us through its difficulty. This truth is beautifully summarized by Mormon when he wrote of Alma's people, who were in bondage and prayed for deliverance: "And now it came to pass that the burdens which were laid upon Alma and his brethren were made light; yea, the Lord did strengthen them that they could bear up their burdens with ease" (Mosiah 24:15). I share the following story with permission from a former university student, Caitlin, to illustrate how Christ can strengthen us, even if the burden remains.

Caitlin told me of her deteriorating relationship with her father who, during her sixth-grade year in school, had begun using cocaine. She wrote, "My mother divorced [my dad] after my seventh-grade year, and from that point up until the beginning of my senior year, it was constant fighting." She wrote of her dad's problems, manipulations, arguments, and his "horrible decisions that were ruining our family." Upon returning home one night the summer before her freshman year, Caitlin's mother broke the news that her father had taken his own life. In the moment of this tragedy, however, Caitlin experienced the strengthening power of Christ:

Sometimes God doesn't eradicate the burden, but He gives us spiritual strength to carry us through its difficulty.

"I felt this overwhelming love and peace come over me, and I knew it was my Savior comforting me. The strange, foreign emotions were still there, but I literally could feel the comfort of my Savior. What was truly remarkable, however, was that I felt zero negative feelings towards my dad. It was the first time I had ever felt that way for any human being before, let alone someone who hurt me and my family as much as he did. All the horrible things he did to me and my family just seemed to completely dissolve. The only emotion I felt for my dad was love. I once heard that charity is a gift from God. I was given that gift the moment I heard those words [that my dad had taken his life]. I was enabled to see my dad the way Christ sees him, and feel of the sweet, pure love He has for him."

In this instance the trial wasn't removed, but Caitlin was given strength in her trial through gifts of the Spirit. Alma illustrates this "spiritual gift" aspect of the strengthening power of Christ when he prayed for the gift of patience: "O Lord God, how long wilt thou suffer that such wickedness and infidelity shall be among this people? O Lord, wilt thou give me strength, that I may bear with mine infirmities. For I am infirm . . . wilt thou grant unto me that I may have strength, that I may suffer with patience these afflictions" (Alma 31:30–31). Because of mortality and human agency, sometimes God won't change circumstances to relieve a burden. *When God can't or won't change an external circumstance, however, he can and will change our internal workings to successfully meet the challenge, if we let him.* He often does this by making our burdens feel lighter through divine spiritual gifts that expand our perspective, empower our understanding, alter our attitude, and provide patience, comfort, and peace.

Strength to Resist Temptation and Overcome Sin

A second aspect of divine strength we can receive is power to resist temptation and overcome sin. This is different than cleansing and healing from sin and transgression; this is a protective power to "suffer us not to be led into temptation" (JST, Matthew 6:13).

Masterful paintings that have been damaged often go through a careful process of cleansing years of dirt and dust buildup, healing rips in the canvas and breaks in the frame, and restoring lost pigment. That is not all, however. There is also an extensive conservation aspect of the cleansed, healed, and restored art: The curators add layers of protective varnish, control temperature and natural light exposure, install security warning systems, and go to great lengths to shield the artwork from future damage. Similarly, Jesus not only cleanses, heals, and restores us from the damaging effects of sin, but his grace also grants daily power to guard and protect us against future damaging disobedience. This strengthening power enables us to resist partaking of "the sin which doth so easily beset us" (Hebrews 12:1) as Paul said. Elder M. Russell Ballard taught: "One of the most devastating effects of sin is that it weakens you, binds you, brings you down to slavery. The grace of God and of His Son, the Lord Jesus Christ, is the answer to that predicament. If you will but humble yourselves and turn to Them, then Their grace, Their enabling power, can not only help you throw off the chains of sin but actually turn your weaknesses into strengths."[8]

Our hymns remind us that "when temptations are before us" God can "give us strength to overcome."[9] There is a divine,

> Jesus not only cleanses, heals, and restores us from the damaging effects of sin, but his grace also grants daily power to guard and protect us against future damaging disobedience.

strengthening power from God available to all of us as we each strive to resist the enemy's enticements. *We are promised that God will always provide a guiding and a protecting influence to help us resist making serious mistakes.*[10] These divine disclaimers may come as a thought to our mind, a feeling to our heart, a vision in our mind's eye, a remembrance, a word from a loved one, an invisible hand to restrain and/or constrain that will strengthen us to do his will and resist the adversary's seductions (*see Study Suggestion 2*). We have our agency and can choose for ourselves, but amidst our common temptations, let us uncommonly remember that "God is faithful, who will not suffer you to be tempted above that ye are able; but will with the temptation also make a way to escape, that ye may be able to bear it" (1 Corinthians 10:13).

Strength to Do Good Works

A third aspect of the strengthening power of Christ is a power that is given to us to do good works beyond our natural capacities. It is a power granted to do miracles, in every sense of the word (see Alma 26:12). The Bible Dictionary teaches: "It is likewise through the grace of the Lord that individuals, through faith in the Atonement of Jesus Christ . . . receive strength and assistance to do good works that they otherwise would not be able to maintain if left to their own means."[11] This gift to do and be good beyond our natural capacity is perhaps most evident in church callings and assignments. Ironically, or perhaps purposefully, most of us are called to serve in church positions for which we are utterly unqualified. No formal training in religious pedagogy? No problem, come teach the Gospel Doctrine class! Social phobia? Let's assign you three families to home teach. Can't manage your own finances? We'd like to call you to be the ward clerk. Get easily frustrated by your children? Then come model Jesus's love and patience as a Primary worker! Terrible note-taker? Secretary in the presidency for you. You say you're not a natural leader? Well, the Lord would like you to be the bishop.

With regard to our church callings, however, the ever-quotable Elder Neal A. Maxwell taught: "God does not begin by asking us about our ability, but only about our availability, and if we then prove our dependability, he will increase our capability."[12] Those of us who have offered the Lord our personal five loaves and two fishes and placed them in his marvelous hands have watched him multiply our capacity to feed thousands [13] with basketfuls left over (see John 6:9–12). *Each week in wards across the earth, the strengthening power of Christ is manifest in millions of persons performing and doing good works beyond their natural capacity as the Lord qualifies them through endowments of his enabling grace.*

Beyond callings, the strengthening power of Christ is available *for any worthy work we might undertake:* whether doctor or dentist, scientist or researcher, teacher or student, artist or entertainer, businessperson or construction worker, athlete or mathlete. Above all, divine strength to do good works is given for the daily, eternally important work of families: to spouses, parents, and children, each of whom is striving to perform a work beyond their natural capacities. One of my favorite parental sayings is, "Before I got married I had six theories about bringing up children; now I have six children and no theories."[14] I have prayed for and kindly received special helps and strengths from the Lord in my own life's work in my family, church service, and career. As I write this very chapter, I pray for

God to strengthen me in my weakness. Over and over again, God has kindly strengthened me as I have sought him in faith, as he has mercifully done for countless others.

The same power that strengthened Peter to walk on water is the same power that can strengthen you to accomplish amazing things. The power that enabled Mary the mother of Jesus to bear and care for the Son of God is the very power that divinely enables mothers the world over to bear and care for God's other beloved children. By Jesus's grace, inspiration is given, ideas are communicated, energy is awarded, persistence is provided, wisdom is revealed, answers are shown, and gifts are bestowed—all so God's children might perform good works and do well. This power to do good beyond our natural capacity is available for every worthy work every day. The First Presidency has promised: "The Lord will make much more out of your life than you can by yourself. He will increase your opportunities, expand your vision, and strengthen you."[15]

> **The same power that strengthened Peter to walk on water is the same power that can strengthen you to accomplish amazing things.**

Receiving Strength through Weakness

As with many of Christ's teachings, there is a paradox in the process of receiving divine strength: it comes through admitted weakness. *Just as true freedom only comes through submissive obedience (John 5:39), true strength only comes through acknowledging true dependence.* The Apostle Paul said that his "strength is made perfect in weakness. Most gladly therefore will I rather glory in my infirmities [weaknesses], that the power of Christ may rest upon me. . . . For when I am weak, then am I strong" (2 Corinthians 12:9–10). I am impressed with how Alcoholics Anonymous fully employs the paradoxical idea of strength through weakness. The very first step in their twelve-step program articulates the theology of dependence: "We admitted we were powerless over alcohol—that our lives had become unmanageable" and then, step two: "Came to believe that a Power greater than ourselves could restore us to sanity."[16] Our own LDS-adapted version, the Addiction Recovery Program, uses almost the same language in their twelve steps,[17] teaching that "as you yield your heart to God and *grow stronger in humility,* your resolve not to repeat past behaviors will become firmer and firmer."[18] "Stronger in humility" is not a contradiction—it's a gospel truth. Divine strength in any form is received through humble, utter dependence upon God.

Author and LDS philosopher Adam Miller calls this a "hermeneutics of weakness." Hermeneutics is all about interpretation, and one of Brother Miller's interpretations bolsters this concept that strength only comes through weakness: "Rather than abolishing human weakness, grace reveals that our original and essential weakness is the point at which God's saving strength intervenes in our lives."[19] Miller continues: "Weakness names our createdness, our lack of autonomous sovereignty, our persistent dependence on God and his grace for life and agency. In short, weakness names our essential relatedness to God and, thus, our unity with him. . . . To confess our weakness is to confess our connection to him. It follows, then, that if we are humble and acknowledge our insufficiency, his grace will be sufficient. The only thing that could prevent the sufficiency of his grace is our refusal to admit a need for it."[20]

Much like the Apostle Peter's first encounter with the Lord, we can only receive Christ's strengthening power when we seek him in an attitude of dependence. Peter, an expert and professional fisherman who had fished all night long and caught nothing on his own may have been hesitant to turn to a carpenter and traveling preacher for fishing advice when he, seemingly randomly, told him where to drop his net. Peter, with an air of self-sufficiency, tells Jesus, "Master, we have toiled all the night, and have taken nothing." Notice, then, the catalyzing word, the turn in humble submissiveness to Christ: "*Nevertheless* at thy word I will let down the net. And when they had this done, they inclosed a great multitude of fishes: and their net brake" (Luke 5:5–6; emphasis added). When we trust in the arm of the flesh (see 2 Nephi 4:34), pridefully rely upon our own wisdom and strength (see Helaman 16:15), and think we are wise, knowing of ourselves (see 2 Nephi 9:28), we dam the waters of Christ's enabling grace (*see Study Suggestion 3*). *Conversely, when we trust in God, humbly approach him in our admitted weakness, and turn to him for the answers, it opens the floodgates of grace and causes a surge of divine strength.* Thus, as Moroni was taught by Christ, "My grace is sufficient for all men that humble themselves before me; for if they humble themselves before me, and have faith in me, then will I make weak things become strong unto them" (Ether 12:27). Admitting our weakness to God is exactly what enables Christ to strengthen us: "*And because thou has seen thy weakness* thou shalt be made strong" (Ether 12:37; emphasis added). Self-sufficiency and independence, while virtues, are antithetical to actuating grace. Conscious, dependent humility is the very thing that will help us receive Christ's strengthening grace in our daily life.

If the Lord Has Such Great Power

I conclude this chapter where I began—with Nephi. When his brothers mocked him and challenged his ability to build a ship to cross the ocean, Nephi recounted how Moses and the children of Israel were "led forth by his matchless power into the land of promise" (1 Nephi 17:42), and he rebuked his brothers for not believing that God could similarly lead them. And then, Nephi preached a sermon of strengthening poetry:

"And it came to pass that I, Nephi, said unto them that they should murmur no more against their father; neither should they withhold their labor from me, for God had commanded me that I should build a ship.

"And I said unto them: If God had commanded me to do all things I could do them. If he should command me that I should say unto this water, be thou earth, it should be earth; and if I should say it, it would be done.

"And now, if the Lord has such great power, and has wrought so many miracles among the children of men, how is it that he cannot instruct me, that I should build a ship?" (1 Nephi 17:49–51).

If the Lord has such great power . . . how is it that he cannot instruct me? That same statement or question should resonate in the mind of all who truly believe in the grace and strengthening power of Jesus Christ. If God has given so much power, deliverance, and strength to countless disciples in varied situations across all generations, how is it that he cannot give it to us today? Why can't he give me strength to meet my challenges and bear my burdens? How is it that Jesus cannot give me power to resist daily temptations and overcome sin? If the Lord has helped so many people in the past do so many marvelous works, how is it that he cannot help me to do good works beyond my natural capacity? The truth is, if we seek him today, acknowledging our weakness to receive his strength, through his daily grace he can and he will. Through the strengthening power of Christ we can be given "strength such as is not known among men" (D&C 24:12).

Further Study Suggestions: The Strengthening Power

Study Suggestion 1: Examples of divine strength

• Study Nephi's five thesis statement stories and look for the strengthening power of Christ in each of them:

(a) The Fleeing (1 Nephi 1–2)   (d) The Liahona (1 Nephi 16)

(b) The Plates (1 Nephi 3)   (e) The Women (1 Nephi 17)

(c) The Binding (1 Nephi 7)

• I listed a handful of scriptural examples of when God gave strength to bear burdens, resist temptation, or do great works. Which additional scriptural stories come to your mind to illustrate the strengthening power of Christ? When have you been strengthened in some way by God? If you haven't recorded that personal experience, record it for your and/or your future posterity's benefit.

Study Suggestion 2: Strength to resist temptation

• Study Moses 1 to see how he received strength to resist the adversary. What do you learn from his experience?

• Even Jesus was strengthened to remain obedient and resist temptation. Read Matthew 4:1–11 and look for what helped strengthen Christ to resist temptation in this instance. Specifically verses 2, 4, 7, 10, and the Joseph Smith translation in footnote 5a. Ponder how you can follow the Savior's example to help receive strength to resist the temptations that trouble you.

• Jesus struggled in the Garden of Gethsemane under the atoning weight of his suffering. Luke is the only gospel author who tells us that "there appeared an angel unto him from heaven, strengthening him" (Luke 22:43). How has the ministering of angels strengthened you to resist temptation and be obedient? How can you better avail yourself of ministering angels to help strengthen you against sin? Study 2 Nephi 32:3; Moroni 4–5; 7:36–37; and D&C 13 for potential insights into the ministering of angels and how to receive their strengthening power.

Study Suggestion 3: Weakness and strength

• Some of us do not rely upon or access Christ's strengthening power as we should. Read D&C 30:1 and highlight the Lord's rebuke of David Whitmer for his lack of looking to the Lord for help. How can well-intended messages such as being a strong person or being independent and self-sufficient be detrimental to the concept of weakness in seeking the Lord's strengthening power and help?

• Sometimes we hear in church classes or other settings the sentiment that "God won't give you more than you can handle," often citing 1 Corinthians 10:13. How may that sentiment be contextually or doctrinally inaccurate? Why would God allow us to experience more than we can handle on our own? How is despair often a catalyst for strengthening grace?

• The Apostle Paul spoke often about how Christ strengthened him in his weakness. What were Paul's weaknesses—or his "thorn in the flesh"—that he often spoke of? Study Romans 7:14–24 and 2 Corinthians 2:7–10. How did Paul's admitted weakness enable Jesus's strengthening grace? How can admitting weakness enable it for you? What may keep you from truly admitting to God your weaknesses and humbly seeking dependence upon him?

THE TRANSFORMING POWER OF CHRIST

One of the themes of Victor Hugo's *Les Misérables* that has resonated through the years is the question of whether or not people's natures can change, with the character of Jean Valjean representing that question. Is a man who was unjustly imprisoned and thereby became a criminal *always* a criminal, bitter and angry for life? Are our flaws forever? Our immorality irreversible? Our pride permanent? Our selfishness set in stone? Some, like Inspector Javert, say yes: "Men like me can never change. Men like you can never change," he tells Valjean. However, like the priest who knows better, the Son of God emphatically says otherwise. King Benjamin tells us that through Christ's divine powers we can put off "the natural man" and become a "saint through the atonement of Christ the Lord, . . . submissive, meek, humble, patient, full of love" (Mosiah 3:19). Our Lord tells us that because of his grace our very nature and character can be changed, redeemed, converted, reborn, and made new to exemplify his divine image and character. "Therefore if any man be in Christ, he is a new creature: old things are passed away; behold, all things are become new" (2 Corinthians 5:17). The highest and holiest purposes of the Atonement of Jesus Christ—the transforming power—miraculously can do just that.

Chapter 6

THE TRANSFORMING POWER OF CHRIST

The gospel of Jesus Christ is a gospel of transformation.
It takes us as men and women of the earth and
refines us into men and women for the eternities.
—Elder Joseph B. Wirthlin

On first read, Jesus's first recorded miracle may seem a bit trivial. At a wedding feast in Cana of Galilee, the Lord turned dirty water into festive wine. In comparison to his later miracles that were deeply moving—cleansing leprosy, healing the blind, raising a young woman from death—this miracle, which seemingly achieved nothing more than to awe a few servants and further enliven a party, seems almost beneath him. Yet there he is, granting his mother's appeal to divinely provide wine at a party. Of all the miracles Jesus could have done, why did he make this inconsequential request the first public display of his power? Why not do something, frankly, more meaningful? However, the more I ponder the miracle of water to wine, the more I see it as perhaps the most fitting of the "beginning of miracles" (John 2:11) from which Jesus could have taught us the ultimate purpose of his life, mission, and divine power.

It was customary in Jewish tradition for a person to wash his or her hands before eating (see Mark 7:3; Luke 11:37–38), and that if he or she were deemed "unclean" by the law of Moses because of bleeding, leprosy, or disease, anything touched without clean hands was also considered unclean: "And whomsoever he toucheth that hath the issue [of Mosaic uncleanliness], and hath not rinsed his hands in water . . . be unclean" (Leviticus 15:11). Thus, observant

Jews would ceremonially wash their hands before and after most activities, including before eating at a party or a wedding. The six large water pots that, presumably, sat at the door of the wedding at Cana were there for the attendees to wash their hands "after the manner of the purifying of the Jews" (John 2:6)—so they would be both physically and ritually clean. Needless to say, although the pots held a lot of water—two or three firkins apiece according to John (about 100 to 150 gallons total)—after dozens of

Jesus used the miracle of turning water into wine to send the profound message that he had the power to change the very nature of things—to transform not just the state of liquids, but the state of lives.

ceremonial hand washings, those weren't vessels from which you would want to take a long drink, let alone pour the party wine.

Yet Jesus chose those murky, filthy, bacteria-laced water pots for this miracle, and asked the servants to fill them to the brim. Using his divine power, he turned water from those unclean vessels into the finest, best wine of the night (see John 2:10). And therein lies the heavenly lesson: Jesus used the miracle of turning water into wine to send the profound message that he had the power to change the very nature of things—to transform not just the state of liquids, but the state of lives. "Don't you see?" he could have said to the amazed servants afterward, "I can take dirty things and make them clean. I can take everyday elements and make them exceptional. I can take things into my hands and change them. And if you come unto me, I can do the same for you. I can take you and transform you from a natural person into a heavenly saint. That's why I am here. That's what I have power to do." Now, tell me if that is not a great first miracle after all.

Transformation: The Highest Purpose of Life

"Like water to wine, from human to divine" can summarize the entire purpose of our mortal existence and relationship with Christ. President David O. McKay said the core "purpose of the gospel" is "to change human nature."[1] Implying this fundamental concept, another title used for the plan of salvation is the "plan of redemption" (see Alma 12:26, 30, 32–33; 17:16; 18:39). Redeeming something implies more than just saving something. *Redeem* implies "buy back," "repurchase," or "change for the better."[2] While redemption could be understood as Christ exchanging his suffering for ours or buying back our punishment from justice, the plan of redemption could also rightfully be interpreted as the Father's plan, through Christ, to exchange and improve our character; that Christ's divinity exchanges, changes, and remakes us as individuals. This is more than just a plan of salvation, of rescue. It's a plan of rebirth. A plan of conversion. A plan of transformation—but a plan to transform us into what, exactly? Incredibly, into someone more like God (*see Study Suggestion 1*).

Joseph Smith taught, "God himself, finding he was in the midst of spirits and glory, because he was more intelligent, saw proper to institute laws whereby the rest could have a privilege to advance like himself."³ The First Presidency summarized this concept thus: "In the premortal existence, Heavenly Father prepared a plan to enable us to become like Him."⁴ Or, in the sublime summation by Lorenzo Snow: "As man now is, God once was; as God is now man may be."⁵ *The Father's ultimate purpose for implementing the plan of redemption is so that we can become like him. It is more than just living with God, it is living like God; being given not just all that he has, but all that he is.* God wants us to have eternal life, which literally means to have "God's life"⁶ (see D&C 19:4–10). Lowercase "g" gods is how the Doctrine and Covenants explains our reward (see D&C 76:58; 132:20). Heaven won't just be sitting around on celestial clouds singing worship songs or praise music for eternity. The highest form of worship is emulation, and we will worship God in heaven by living as He does—acting, thinking, doing, loving, teaching, serving, and creating like Him in a celestial family with an immortal body of flesh and bone. Mortality provides us the opportunity to learn and grow and prepare for this future state—our time not only "to prepare to meet God" (Alma 34:32), but to prepare to become more like him. That is "how to worship" (D&C 93:19) according to the Lord. "For if you keep my commandments you shall receive of his fulness, and be glorified in me as I am in the Father; therefore, I say unto you, you shall receive grace for grace" (D&C 93:20).

Being Born Again

Like all things, Jesus acts as an intermediary between us and heaven in the process of becoming more like our Father in Heaven. Each day as we experience and receive the Savior's influence and power in our personal lives, whether through being forgiven, or healed, or helped, it has a powerful effect upon our character. Repetitive daily contact with Christ is like sandpaper to the soul that eventually smooths and polishes a celestial character. Christ's divine influence helps us to grow from bad to decent, from decent to good, from good to great, and one day—because of him—from great to a god. Or, in the words of Peter, through Jesus we have "exceeding great and precious promises: that . . . ye might be partakers of the divine nature" (2 Peter 1:4). Christ has promised that through his divinity we can become celestial—heavenly wine, no matter what kind of unclean mortal water we may currently be.

Repetitive daily contact with Christ is like sandpaper to the soul that eventually smooths and polishes a celestial character.

In scriptural language this transformative change toward God through Christ's influence is sometimes called conversion (see Alma 27:25; Helaman 6:3–4; 3 Nephi 9:20; Luke 22:32; Acts 15:3). Although the word *conversion* can be synonymous with the act of accepting Christ or the event of baptism, true conversion is much more than that. It is a Christ-centered change of heart, desires, attitude, behavior, and character. *Conversion isn't a one-time experience or something that happens overnight, but is the cumulative effect of our continual coming unto Christ and being perfected by him.* The Church publication *True to the Faith* states: "Conversion includes a change in behavior, but it goes beyond behavior; it is a change in our very nature. It is such a significant change that the Lord and His prophets refer to it as a rebirth, a change of heart."[7] Sometimes this transformative, converting change is called being "born again" (*see Study Suggestion 2*).

We all have known people, or perhaps have experienced it ourselves, who have undergone this miracle of transforming rebirth. Whether or not you agree with his politics, I was impressed with the testimony that an aspiring US presidential candidate, then–Texas governor George W. Bush, gave during a 1999 Republican primary debate. When the moderator asked the candidates what "political philosopher or thinker" they identified with most, some candidates cited notable statesmen such as Abraham Lincoln or Ronald Reagan. Bush, the third candidate to answer, didn't hesitate and answered straightly, "Christ, because he changed my heart." When moderator John Bachman pressed him to explain how Christ had changed his heart, Bush replied: "When you turn your heart and your life over to Christ, when you accept Christ as the savior, it changes your heart. It changes your life. And that's what happened to me."[8] While some might read political calculation in his response, Bush's sincerity is plainly evident on the video recording. When he finished, the highly evangelical Iowa audience cheered and applauded loudly, and as believers in spiritual rebirth, so should we.

A person experiencing the transforming power of Christ has such "a mighty change" wrought by Jesus's divinity upon them that over time he or she has "no more *disposition* to do evil, but to do good continually" (Mosiah 5:2; emphasis added). It's not that converted people don't sin, but, like Lamoni's people, "their hearts [have] been changed; that they [have] no more *desire* to do evil" (Alma 19:33; emphasis added). A rebellious disposition is replaced by a righteous disposition. A selfish bent is overturned by a selfless one. A slothful "maybe I'll do the minimum of what you want me to do" is completely swallowed up by an attitude of devotion, wanting to be anxiously engaged in good things, particularly in serving God and serving others around them (see D&C 58:26–27). In the iconic words of King Benjamin, the "natural man" has been transformed by "the atonement of Christ the Lord," and has been converted spiritually into "a child, submissive, meek, humble, patient, full of love, willing to submit to all things" (Mosiah 3:19). In a born-again person, the natural man is ousted from his tyrannical seat within us by the democracy of grace, and Godlike transformation reigns instead.

> In a born-again person, the natural man is ousted from his tyrannical seat within us by the democracy of grace, and Godlike transformation reigns instead.

Conversion Is a Process

Notably, this internal revolution takes time. Nations aren't liberated overnight—and freed nations still battle to maintain liberty. Individually exiling the adversary takes similar effort, time, divine aid, and continued diligence. While the scriptures contain multiple examples of people who radically changed (apparently very quickly, such as Alma the Younger), remember that those are exceptions, not the rule. It's almost as if the Lord uses them to make a drastic point. *Most Godlike transformation comes subtly, slowly, almost imperceptibly.*[9] The Lord reminds us "in *due time* [we will] receive of his fulness" (D&C 93:19; emphasis added). We live in a fast-food, instant-answer, "great abs in thirty days!" society, and we can get disillusioned if we don't become spiritually fit overnight. That isn't how spiritual conversion happens. Elder D. Todd Christofferson taught: "You may ask, Why doesn't this mighty change happen more quickly with me? . . . For most of us, the changes are more gradual and occur over time. Being born again, unlike our physical birth, is more a process than an event."[10]

Thus, one might lament, "I know I shouldn't, but I lose my patience with my kids!" Another might say, "I want to be a better person and loving like Christ, but I still find myself being critical of my family and friends." Someone else may say, "I don't want to do this sin. I want to be obedient. But I keep slipping up and I hate it." The mere fact that you are thinking those things shows Christ is working in you, showing your weakness, and conversion is happening. Don't give up, and don't lose hope. Remember, spiritual transformation through Christ is described in scripture with words like *patience, diligence,* and *long-suffering* (see Alma 32:43). Great things take time, effort, oft-repeated failures, and persistence. To behold "the glory of the Lord" and then be "changed into the same image from glory to glory," as he is (2 Corinthians 3:18), is a lifelong pursuit. It takes years of immersing ourselves in the "righteous cycle" (as opposed to the "pride cycle"), of seeking to do God's will in faith, repenting of our failings, committing to him by covenant, and striving to receive of his Spirit—and then doing this over and over and over again.[11] Peter says this continued process purifies "your souls in obeying the truth through the Spirit," resulting in "being born again" (1 Peter 1:22–23).

Rebirth Isn't Something You Do— It's Done to You

Some may read the preceding paragraphs and disagree, saying, "I don't think that can happen to me. I think this is just the way I am. I try to change and just fail. I've read all the self-help books. I've been to countless classes and conferences. I've even tried yoga. No matter how hard I try, I can't change myself." And you know what? That's true. *You* can't. One paradox of being spiritually reborn or converted is that you cannot do it yourself. *You can no more rebirth yourself spiritually than you can birth yourself mortally. It isn't something we do ourselves, it is something that is done to us by Christ.* In a 1672 work by the Puritan pastor Joseph Alleine, published after his death, we read, "Conversion then, in short, lies in the thorough change both of the heart and life. . . . If ever you would be savingly converted, you must despair of doing it in your own strength. It is a resurrection from the dead (Eph. 2:1), a new creation (Gal. 6:15; Eph. 2:10), a work of absolute omnipotence (Eph. 1:19). Are not these out of the reach of human power? . . . [Conversion] is a supernatural work."[12]

Spiritual transformation is different than trying to be a better person. We don't merely, Benjamin Franklin–like, make a list of all the virtues we want to acquire and then focus on them one-by-one until we have perfected them in our lives.[13] As noble as personal improvement efforts like these are, we don't need Christ nor his gospel for that. Otherwise we should just go to the self-improvement section in the bookstore instead of the Savior. No, similar to our first birth, our converting, transforming spiritual rebirth is brought about by heavenly factors beyond our own control. Nowhere does Jesus teach this more plainly than in John 3 when he interviews—or humbles—the great Pharisee teacher Nicodemus. Jesus wastes no time and cuts right to the heart of an issue which he discerns Nicodemus doesn't understand: "Verily, verily, I say unto thee, Except a man be born again, he cannot see the kingdom of God" (John 3:3). This saying may well have rattled Nicodemus who, as a legalistic, checklist Pharisee perhaps thought that salvation came by strict adherence to the pharisaical rituals and extrapolations of the Law of Moses—things that he did and controlled. But being born again? This was beyond him.

Sensing the profound implications of what Christ has just said to him, Nicodemus asks in return, "How can a man be born when he is old? can he enter the second time into his mother's womb, and be born?" (John 3:4). Here we must give Nicodemus some credit. This famous teacher[14] in Israel was not, as we sometimes hear taught in church classes, actually thinking he had to literally reenter his mother's womb to be born again. He was actually picking up on Jesus's use of birth as a spiritual metaphor and saying, "How is it possible for me to change? I can't change myself. Especially as I'm an old man now. I am who I am. I might as well try to go back into my mother's womb as well as try to make myself become a new person. This is impossible!" And Jesus's answer was that, yes, it is impossible—on your own. You've got to be born of the Spirit, Nicodemus! The Lord adds, "Except a man be born of water and of the Spirit, he cannot enter into the kingdom of God" (John 3:5). While we may control if and when we are baptized by water, we don't control the cleansing and sanctifying influence of the Holy Ghost upon us. It is a gift from God, something that isn't earned or dictated, just freely sent and received. Thus the *gift* of the Holy Ghost—a gift of grace.

Jesus illustrates this with a metaphor: "The wind bloweth where it listeth, and thou hearest the sound thereof, but canst not tell whence it cometh, and whither it goeth: so is every one that is born of the Spirit" (John 3:8). Nicodemus doesn't cause the wind; he experiences it. Nicodemus didn't control his birth; it happened to him. Similarly, just as you and I don't control the element of the wind and its influence upon us, we don't control the elements of heaven and their spiritual effects upon us. We may ask, we may seek, we may desire, and we may strive—of necessity—to place ourselves in the right way to receive of its influence, but like the breeze we aren't in charge of how and when the Spirit comes upon us. Go watch anyone try to fly a kite in the dead calm of a summer's day and see how well that works out. And go watch someone try to become like Jesus without the wind of the Spirit to lift them up and make them soar. It won't happen. You may as well try to birth yourself. You may as well try to turn water to wine. Notice Jesus's use of the word *I* in the promise of born-again change made to Ezekiel: "A new heart also will *I* give you, and a new spirit will *I* put within you: and *I* will take away the stony heart out of your flesh, and *I* will give you an heart of flesh. And *I* will put my spirit within you" (Ezekiel 36:26–27; emphasis added). Transformation is a spiritual gift from God, not an accomplishment earned by our efforts. That's an important lesson that Christ wanted not just Nicodemus to understand, but all of us. It causes us to be humble seekers and receivers, not prideful earners and accomplishers.

Transformed through Charity

There is a reason why conversion is termed "being born of the Spirit" (Mosiah 27:24). The Holy Ghost and its attendant spiritual gifts delivers to us the grace of Christ and helps bring about our spiritual rebirth and transformation. President George Q. Cannon taught: "If any of us are imperfect, it is our duty to pray for the gift that will make us perfect. Have I imperfections? I am full of them. What is my duty? To pray to God to give me the gifts that will correct these imperfections. If I am an angry man, it is my duty to pray for charity, which suffereth long and is kind. Am I an envious man? It is my duty to seek for charity, which envieth not. So with all the gifts of the Gospel. They are intended for this purpose. No man ought to say, 'Oh, I cannot help this; it is my nature.' He is not justified in it, for the reason that God has promised to give strength to correct these things, and to give gifts that will eradicate them."[15]

While all spiritual influence helps to touch our hearts and change our characters, perhaps no spiritual gift is greater than the gift of charity for its transforming influence and effect upon who we are and become. Notice in the preceding quote how George Q. Cannon twice refers to the gift of charity as the solution for converting the natural man. Paul says, "Now abideth faith, hope, charity, these three; but the greatest of these is charity"

(1 Corinthians 13:13). Or, as Mormon said, "Wherefore, cleave unto charity, which is the greatest of all" (Moroni 7:46). To understand how and why charity is so central to spiritual rebirth and transformation, we must first correctly understand what the spiritual gift of charity is—and is not.

Defining Charity

Sometimes the definition of the gift of charity is overly simplified as "service" or "loving others." Although lovingly feeding the hungry, visiting the sick, and taking care of the poor and needy are necessary Christlike actions and the essence of "pure religion" (James 1:27), they are not the divine gift of charity. The Bible Dictionary says that in the scriptures "[Charity] is never used to denote alms or deeds of benevolence."[16] Charity is a small English word that encompasses a large heavenly concept. Originally the word was *agapē*, which is Greek for "the love of God for man and of man for God."[17] Nearly all cases in the English New Testament where the word *charity* is used, it is translated from *agapē*—the love of God for us and our love for him in return. The Book of Mormon uses it the same way: "And again, I remember that thou hast said that thou [Jesus] hast loved the world, even unto the laying down of thy life for the world . . . And now I know that this love which thou hast had for the children of men is charity" (Ether 12:33–34).

Thus, first and foremost the definition of charity is God's love for his children, or the love *of* God. But charity is a two-fold reciprocal gift. The second aspect of the gift of charity is returning that love back toward God, or love *for* God. "We love him, because he first loved us" (1 John 4:19), John taught. If we read the scriptures carefully, we find that these two definitions of charity—God loving us, and us loving God—are how charity is used (*see Study Suggestion 3*). Notice how Alma replaced the word *charity* with "the love of God" when he said, "Having faith on the Lord; having a hope that ye shall receive eternal life; having the love of God always in your hearts" (Alma 13:29). The spiritual gift of charity is bestowed when God manifests his divine love to us and we receive it, and we reciprocate our love to God in our heart, mind, and actions. Thus,

Charity: God's love for us + our love for God = loving others like God.

charity is a loving relationship with God. It is when, as a gift from heaven, God says, "I love you," and out of experiencing that divine love, our natural reply to God is, "I love you too." *The spiritual gift of charity is a condition, not an action. It is something we receive, not give. Charity is not what we do to others, it's what God does to us.* When we experience the love of God, however, it does do something to us. Not only do we love God in return, but his love causes us to love his other children too. As Lehi did, when we partake of the fruit of the love of God it causes us, as a spiritual byproduct, to instinctively turn toward others (see 1 Nephi 8:12). Charity is God's love for us + our love for God = loving others like God.

Receiving Charity

When God says, "I love you," and we experience charity, that gift brings about transforming effects in our character and lives. After the resurrected Savior appeared in the Americas, "the people were all *converted* unto the Lord, upon all the face of the land" (4 Nephi 1:2) and "there was no contention in the land, *because of the love of God* which did dwell in the hearts of the people" (4 Nephi 1:15; emphasis added). Charity converted them, and charity changed them. When Mormon spoke of charity in Moroni 7, it seems he was not defining charity but describing the transforming *effects* of the love of God upon us—the fruits of what happens to us when we receive charity. A person who experiences the gift of charity "suffereth long, and is kind, and envieth not, and is not puffed up, seeketh not her own, is not easily provoked, thinketh no evil, and rejoiceth not in iniquity but rejoiceth in the truth, beareth all things, believeth all things, hopeth all things, endureth all things" (Moroni 7:45). In other words, a person who experiences charity is changed and transformed.

President Dieter F. Uchtdorf connected transformation with receiving the gift of charity: "This 'mighty change' of heart is exactly what the gospel of Jesus Christ is designed to bring into our lives. How is it done? Through the love of God."[18] Elder M. Russell Ballard similarly counseled, "Ask to be filled with the power of Christ's pure love. You may have to do this many times, but I testify to you that your body, mind, and spirit can be transformed."[19] Thus, to receive the gift of charity we must "pray unto the Father with all the energy of heart, that ye may be filled with this love," which God promises to bestow "upon all who are true followers of his Son, Jesus Christ" (Moroni 7:48). When we pray to the Father and seek to receive the gift of charity—God's love—we are also seeking to receive Jesus (see Moroni 7:44). You can't feel the various powers of Christ—cleansing, healing, restoring, identifying, strengthening,

> Like rocks in a river, when the heavenly influence of charity continually washes over someone, its celestial current rounds the rough and stony edges, smooths them, and spiritually polishes them.

transforming—without feeling God's love, because Jesus Christ is the perfect manifestation of God's love (see John 3:16).

Charity isn't a one-time encounter, either. Experiencing the love of God must happen over and over. As in a marriage, our covenant love with God must be experienced and renewed consistently throughout our lives, even daily. Therefore we should seek out those things that help us feel God's love today. As Alma asked, "If ye have experienced a change of heart, and if ye have felt to sing the song of redeeming love, I would ask, can ye feel so now?" (Alma 5:26). *Feeling love changes people, and repeatedly feeling divine love divinely changes people.* Like rocks in a river, when the heavenly influence of charity continually washes over someone, its celestial current rounds the rough and stony edges, smooths them, and spiritually polishes them.[20] Receiving charity is a key spiritual gift to enable conversion, rebirth, and born-again transformation. Charity is the greatest of all the gifts of God, because it is the greatest in helping us become like God.

Conclusion: The Divine Powers of Christ

Just as the Lord Jesus Christ is more powerful than death, or sin, or Satan, or the winds and the waves, the power of Jesus Christ is more powerful than our natures. President Gordon B. Hinckley said directly, "This gospel . . . can change our very natures."[21] Although the miracles that Jesus repeatedly performed throughout his life were each divine, maybe nothing is more miraculous than the change that is wrought in a person's very character when they are transformed by the power of Christ. Elder John A. Widtsoe said, "I have come to understand that perhaps the greatest miracle in the gospel of the Lord Jesus Christ is the transformation that comes to a man or a woman who in faith accepts the truth of the gospel and who then lives it in his or her life . . . [becoming] transformed from ordinary men into new powers and possibilities."[22] *Regardless of our current character flaws, Christ can refine and eventually transform us into men and women fit for the eternities. If we don't believe that, then we don't believe Jesus.*

Ultimately, all of the powers of Christ discussed in this book are centered on our divine transformation. Why are we cleansed? To become pure, to become like God. Why are we healed? So we will become one with God in body, mind, and spirit. Why are we restored? So that after a sowing and growing season to change and progress and become more Christlike, we can eventually be resurrected to life and find ourselves like God. Why are we identified and empathized with? So we can learn to submit to God's wisdom above our own and do, say, and become what he would have us become. Why are we strengthened? To bear trials successfully, resist and overcome sin, and perform good works beyond our natural capacity, each of which makes us better than what we currently are and enables growth and progression. Like soil and water and sun, the cumulative everyday powers of Christ are ultimately intended to feed our souls and transform us into mighty trees in the forest of heaven. The transforming power of Christ was purposely saved as the last chapter in this book to emphasize this very point.

There is yet another reason why the transforming power was discussed last, and also the cleansing power first. Not only is inner cleansing the first and basic element of spirituality, and transforming the ultimate purpose, but the listed order of all the powers in this book is instructionally intentional. As you may have already deduced, the powers of Christ discussed herein form a memorable acrostic:

Cleansing

Healing

Restoring

Identifying

Strengthening

Transforming

The title of "Christ," which derives from the Greek *Christós,* means "anointed one." Jesus, the Anointed One. Jesus, the one anointed to cleanse, heal, restore, identify, strengthen, and transform. Jesus the Christ. In this sense, the word *Christ* isn't only a name; it's an ever-present power. This sacred title can remind us of the powers he has to offer us on a continual basis if we come unto him and receive him. I don't pretend this acrostic is an all-inclusive list. Clearly, there are other powers of Christ beyond those described in this book. But I believe it represents much of our Lord's divine influence which can affect a disciple's life on a daily basis. Notice each of these powers [in brackets], praised in this psalm of David, and neatly listed in order:

"Bless the Lord, O my soul, and forget not all his benefits: Who forgiveth all thine iniquities [cleansing]; who healeth all thy diseases [healing]; who redeemeth thy life from destruction [re-storing]; who crowneth thee with lovingkindness [identifying] and tender mercies [strengthening]; who satisfieth thy mouth with good things; so that thy youth is renewed like the eagle's [trans-forming]" (Psalm 103:2–5).

Although these powers are interrelated (for example, divine cleansing often is related to divine healing, and vice versa) and can each affect our lives simultaneously, they all lead us to become the children of God and fulfill our divine potential. To bring about this mighty change of heart we must understand, seek, and receive the powers of Christ on a daily basis. As Elder Russell M. Nelson said, "Each day, ours is the challenge to access the power of the Atonement so that we can truly change [and] become more Christlike."[23] As we come unto Christ and receive his divine powers through daily acts related to repentance, faith, sow-ing and growing, prayer, humility, charity, and others, Jesus causes Godlike transformation within us. That's what he does. That's who he is. That's what he promises. We need Jesus more than just when we've sinned or are going through a really difficult trial or when death calls. We need Christ every day, every hour. We continually need his power to cleanse, his power to heal, his power to restore, his power to identify, his power to strengthen, and ultimately his power to transform. This day, we need Jesus. I testify he stands at the door and knocks, even now. May each of us seek his divine powers and grace in our everyday lives.

Christ isn't only a name; it's an ever-present power.

Further Study Suggestions:
The Transforming Power

Study Suggestion 1: The doctrine of deification

• Jesus and others repeatedly suggested that God's children have a divine, Godlike potential. Study the following verses that suggest this: Matthew 5:48; John 10:34; Romans 8:16–17; Philippians 2:5–6; 2 Peter 1:4; D&C 76:58–60; 84:33–39; 93:19–20; 132:19–24.

Study Suggestion 2: Being born again

• Consider how being born again spiritually is similar to being born physically. How is it the same? How is it different? What parallels can you draw? What do you learn from it? Read Moses 6:59–60 and look for the Lord's parallels on the subject to Adam.

• Study the following verses on being born again, or being converted, to see the necessity that the gospel of Jesus Christ is not just about knowing something, but becoming someone: Matthew 18:2; John 3:3; Acts 3:19; Romans 12:2; Mosiah 27:25.

• Study Elder Dallin H. Oaks's classic talk "The Challenge to Become" and ponder on its relationship to the transforming power of Christ.[24]

Study Suggestion 3: Understanding charity

• Read Moroni 7:46–47 but replace each mention of the word *charity* with "the Atonement." "Wherefore, my beloved brethren, if ye have not [the Atonement], ye are nothing, for [the Atonement] never faileth . . ." What does this substitution teach you about the relationship between charity and the love of God and Jesus?

• Find verses that contain the phrase *love of God* (you can search for that phrase in the LDS Gospel Library app or online at scriptures.lds.org). Read those verses but replace *love of God* with "charity." What does it teach you?

• The Prophet Joseph Smith taught: "A [person] filled with the love of God, is not content with blessing his family alone, but ranges through the whole world, anxious to bless the whole human race."[25] When have you experienced charity? If you have not recorded or shared with others significant experiences when you have experienced the love of God, consider how you can do so and act upon it. How has experiencing the love of God caused you to love God and love his children? How can experiencing charity make you a better spouse, parent, friend, or neighbor? What can you do to better seek the gift of charity "with all the energy of heart"? (Moroni 7:48).

Seek this Jesus of whom the prophets and apostles
have written, that the grace of God the Father,
and also the Lord Jesus Christ, and the Holy Ghost,
which beareth record of them, may be and
abide in you forever. Amen.

—Ether 12:41

THE AGENT OF CHRIST'S ATONEMENT: THE HOLY GHOST

In regards to receiving the powers of Christ in our daily lives, an important question remains. The question is beautifully phrased by Enos, when, after his personal experience with the Lord's cleansing power, he asks, almost bewilderedly, "Lord, how is it done?" (Enos 1:7). Although throughout this book I have suggested ways to help receive Jesus's grace in our daily lives, ultimately—like Enos—we may wonder, "But how does grace actually come? How are the powers of Christ delivered into my life?" The answer to these inquiries are found through the third member of the Godhead: The Holy Ghost.

Often when we teach and speak of the Holy Ghost we tend to emphasize his jobs and not necessarily his role. By definition, a *role* is the "why" you do it, and a *job* is the "what" you do to accomplish it. For example, the role of a school principal is to oversee teaching and learning. However, the *jobs* in fulfilling that role are to observe teachers and classrooms, administer budgets, visit with irksome students, and meet with parents. A police officer's role is to protect and to serve. His or her jobs are to arrest criminals, fill out reports, help citizens in need, and write traffic tickets. A mother's role is to nurture God's children. Her jobs are, well, too numerous to even begin making a list.

Similarly, the Holy Ghost has a primary role, and he also has multiple jobs to fulfill that role. The *jobs* of the Holy Ghost (what he does) are many and varied, and usually dominate the majority of our focus in church talks and lessons. For example, we commonly teach that the Holy Ghost guides us, warns us of danger, testifies of divine truth, and comforts us. Those are all true and important. However, those descriptions emphasize his work (what he does), but don't necessarily articulate his central role (why he does it). And if we don't understand the *why* of the Holy Ghost, we miss out on the power available to us that could be evident in our lives.[1] So what is the essential *role* of the Holy Ghost?

The Essential Role of the Holy Ghost

The Godhead consists of three separate beings who have distinct roles yet are one in purpose. Our Heavenly Father's role as the sovereign ruler is to bring to pass the immortality and eternal life of man. Jesus Christ's role is as the Savior and Redeemer, who, through his divine grace, power, and Atonement intercedes for humankind and brings about justification and sanctification in the Father's plan. The primary role of the Holy Ghost is to deliver the blessings and powers of the Atonement of Jesus Christ into our daily lives. In fact, when the Holy Ghost is with us and we feel his divine influence, the Atonement of Jesus Christ is operating within us. President Henry B. Eyring taught, "If you have felt the influence of the Holy Ghost today, you may take it as evidence that the Atonement is working in your life. For that reason and many others, you would do well to put yourself in places and in tasks that invite the promptings of the Holy Ghost."[2] On another occasion, President Eyring said, "When [the Holy Ghost] is your companion, you can have confidence that the Atonement is working in your life."[3] Isn't that wonderful? How many people have wondered or been confused about whether Jesus's Atonement was working in their life yet would have been assured with the simple correlating question of, "Well, have you felt the influence of the Spirit recently? If you have, the Atonement is in effect in your life." Elder D. Todd Christofferson of the Quorum of the Twelve said, "The gift of the Holy Ghost . . . is the messenger of grace by which the blood of Christ is applied [to us]."[4] Answering Enos's earlier inquiry: *That* is how it is done. When we understand that the Holy Ghost's role is to be the agent of the Atonement—the deliverer of divinity—then with his constant companionship we can know that the powers of Christ are being applied to our lives. Let's briefly analyze the Holy Ghost's role in delivering each individual aspect of the powers of Christ discussed in this book.

The primary role of the Holy Ghost is to deliver the blessings and powers of the Atonement of Jesus Christ into our daily lives.

The Holy Ghost and Cleansing

I served much of my full-time LDS mission in some very, very poor areas of Bolivia. Many people were nearly destitute and rarely had the blessing of being able to bathe regularly. I once had one sweet Bolivian boy ask me in sincerity if he could bring some shampoo to his baptism to wash his hair afterward. Baptism isn't meant to be only a literal cleansing; we know that baptism offers us spiritual purification. The Apostle Paul teaches that when we are "baptized into Jesus Christ . . . our old man is crucified with him, that the body of sin might be destroyed, . . . [being] freed from sin" (Romans 6:3, 6–7). We even sing the Primary song, "I know when I am baptized my wrongs are washed away."[5] The waters of baptism, however, only *represent* the cleansing of sin, just as the emblems of the sacrament are figurative representations of the body and blood of Christ. The true cleansing and purification comes when we are baptized by fire through the reception of the Holy Ghost. Elder Bruce R. McConkie taught:

"Sins are remitted not in the waters of baptism, as we say in speaking figuratively, but when we receive the Holy Ghost. It is the Holy Spirit of God that erases carnality and brings us into a state of righteousness."[6] And, "The actual cleansing of the soul comes when the Holy Ghost is received. The Holy Ghost is a sanctifier whose divine commission is to burn dross and evil out of a human soul as though by fire."[7]

Did you catch that? *It is the Holy Ghost that cleanses our sins, purifies, and ultimately sanctifies us.* Elder Christofferson said plainly that "The Holy Ghost . . . will bring relief and forgiveness."[8] Take a look at these scriptures linking the Lord's power of cleansing with the reception of the Holy Ghost:

- "For the gate by which ye should enter is repentance and baptism by water; and *then cometh a remission of your sins by fire and by the Holy Ghost*" (2 Nephi 31:17; emphasis added).
- "Declare . . . remission of sins by baptism, and by fire, yea, *even the Holy Ghost*" (D&C 19:31; emphasis added).
- "Repent, all ye ends of the earth, and come unto me and be baptized in my name, *that ye may be sanctified by the reception of the Holy Ghost,* that ye may stand spotless before me at the last day" (3 Nephi 27:20; emphasis added).

And this isn't just restoration doctrine. The Apostle Paul referred to the Holy Ghost as a cleanser and purifier multiple times in the New Testament as well:

- "That the offering up of the Gentiles might be acceptable, being *sanctified by the Holy Ghost*" (Romans 15:16; emphasis added).
- "But ye are washed, but ye are sanctified, but ye are justified in the name of the Lord Jesus, and *by the Spirit of our God*" (1 Corinthians 6:11; emphasis added).

But perhaps my favorite verse that clearly articulates the cleansing power of the Holy Ghost comes from the Book of Mormon:

- "And after they had been received unto baptism, *and were wrought upon and cleansed by the power of the Holy Ghost,* they were numbered among the people of the church of Christ" (Moroni 6:4; emphasis added).

President Henry B. Eyring said, "Reception of the Holy Ghost is the cleansing agent as the Atonement purifies you."[9] I love that phrase: the "cleansing agent," which is exactly what the Bible Dictionary calls him.[10] On another occasion, President Eyring said, "The reception of the Holy Ghost cleanses us through the Atonement of Jesus Christ."[11] Thus, the forgiving and cleansing power of Christ is activated in our lives by the reception of the Spirit. This relationship between cleansing and the Holy Ghost is highlighted each week as we repent and recommit to Christ through the ordinance of the sacrament; the attendant blessing is that we "may always have his Spirit to be with" us (D&C 20:77), which Spirit brings the Lord's continual power of cleansing.[12]

The Holy Ghost and Healing

Although I do believe—and have witnessed—the physical healing power of Jesus, I do not pretend to know how it works. What makes a fever break, a fractured hip heal, or a heart begin beating again? Although I don't know how physical healing through Christ happens, the scriptures suggest that the Holy Ghost has a part in the process. Note this informative verse in the Book of Mormon: "And as many as had devils cast out from them, and were healed of their sicknesses and their infirmities, did truly manifest unto the people that *they had been wrought upon by the Spirit of God, and had been healed*"

(3 Nephi 7:22; emphasis added). It is notable that all of the gifts of the Spirit—meaning gifts that come to us by the Spirit of God—mentioned in 1 Corinthians 12, Moroni 10, and D&C 46 all speak of the "gift of healing" (Moroni 10:11). These gifts, including the gift to heal and the gift to be healed, are "given by the manifestations of the Holy Ghost" (Moroni 10:8). We are told of the connection between the healing power of Jesus and the Holy Ghost by Luke, who wrote "how God anointed Jesus of Nazareth *with the Holy Ghost and with power:* who went about do-ing good, and healing all that were oppressed" (Acts 10:38; emphasis added). When the whole multitude sought to touch Jesus, "there went virtue out of him, and healed them

The everyday miracle
of mental, emotional,
and spiritual healing
is delivered by
the Holy Ghost.

all" (Luke 6:19), indicating an intangible spiritual power that enabled the healing.[13] It seems that even the ultimate physical healing—the Resurrection—could be done by the power of the Spirit. Lehi taught that Jesus "layeth down his life according to the flesh, and taketh it again *by the power of the Spirit,* that he may bring to pass the res-urrection of the dead" (2 Nephi 2:8). The Doctrine and Covenants says that those who receive and observe the covenants of priesthood ordinances are "sanctified by the Spirit unto the renewing of their bodies" (D&C 84:33), which is contextually speaking of resurrection. Equally, the everyday miracle of mental, emotional, and spiritual healing (oneness with God in mind, body, and spirit) is also delivered by the Holy Ghost, as the hymn "Let the Holy Spirit Guide" peace-fully teaches (see *Hymns,* no. 143).

When we speak of the spiritual healing of Christ we are usually speaking of the more common functions of the Holy Ghost that work their miracles on our minds and hearts: comforting, calming, reassuring, whispering peace, and sending love. I remember one time as a young man getting into an argument with my parents and being so mad I just wanted to punch something. I stormed down into my room and looked for something to throw as I angrily paced back and forth. The first thing my eyes caught, providentially, was my scriptures sitting by my bedside. And, no, I didn't punch or throw them. But I did sit down in a huff and flipped them open—and that is when something heavenly happened. Something—I don't remember what—caught my eye, and I started reading. Turning pages and looking at cross-references, I got lost in the scriptures for about a half-hour, and as I did so, the rage and anger and frustration I felt in my heart melted away into feelings of peace, love, and joy, which feelings came into my heart by the Holy Ghost (see Galatians 5:22–24). I was somewhat like King Saul, who, depressed, had David come play his harp for him and "the evil spirit departed from him" (1 Samuel 16:23). Although that is a small and seemingly insignificant story, it illustrates how the Lord, through his Holy Spirit, brings us into oneness with him, heals our hearts, soothes our souls, and calms our conscience. The divine work of spiritual healing is exactly that—the Lord working with us through the Spirit.

The Holy Ghost and Restoring

The restoring power of Christ is the Lord's ability to make that which is wrong, right; that which is broken, fixed; that which is dead, alive; that which is unfair, fair. *At its heart, receiving the restoring power of Christ is accomplished through the gift of hope.* Hope is the sure knowledge that the promises of God—fairness, goodness, justice, reward, freedom from the fall of Adam and Eve, forgiveness of sin, and eventually the promise of eternal life—will be rewarded to those who trust in Jesus. Thus, we have "hope through the atonement of Christ" (Moroni 7:41). Like all the gifts of grace, the power of hope is delivered to us by the Holy Ghost. Mormon taught, "Because of meekness and lowliness of heart cometh the visitation of the Holy Ghost, which Comforter filleth with hope" (Moroni 8:26). The word *assurance* is a synonym of *hope*, because hope is sure, steadfast, and unwavering (see Ether 12:4). That assurance—that hope—is a gift of the Spirit of God: "For our gospel came not unto you in word only, but also in power, and in the Holy Ghost, and in much assurance" (1 Thessalonians 1:5). The prophets of the Book of Mormon received hope by "many revelations and the spirit of prophecy; and having all these witnesses we obtain a hope" (Jacob 4:6).

It is the Spirit of God who delivers the water of hope to our thirsty soul in the desert of unfairness. To reassure us of God's restoring promises, it is the Holy Ghost that will "bring all things to your remembrance, whatsoever I [The Lord] have said unto you" (John 14:26). Through visions and whispers and subtle promptings that touch the innermost part of the soul, it is the Holy Ghost who will "shew you things to come" (John 16:13)—future blessings, both grand and small—when all of God's promises will be fulfilled (see Mosiah 5:3) and the restitution of all things will be brought to pass. Although the following is an alternate take on

> It is the Spirit of God who delivers the water of hope to our thirsty soul in the desert of unfairness.

the common interpretation, perhaps the scriptural term "the Holy Spirit of promise" (D&C 76:53) doesn't only ratify or approve our actions and ordinances, but he also does exactly what that title implies: he is the Spirit that confirms to our souls the promised blessings of God, including the promise of eternal life (see D&C 88:3–4). Thus, as Paul says, we "may abound in hope, through the power of the Holy Ghost" (Romans 15:13). The restoring power of Jesus—the power and its attendant promises that all will be made right—are confirmed in our souls by the Spirit.

The Holy Ghost and Identifying

Central to delivering the identifying power of Christ (his ability to empathize with us, comfort us, and guide us perfectly) is the Lord's ability to communicate his thoughts and feelings to us. Those divine thoughts and feelings come to our mind and heart by the power of the Holy Ghost (see D&C 8:2–3). In the midst of our pleadings to God for help and guidance in our unique situations, it is the Spirit of God who delivers Jesus's soothing empathetic voice that says, "I understand," "I know," "Let me teach you," and "I will guide you in what to do." The scriptures teach us that it is the Holy Ghost that is "the Comforter" (John 14:26). He is the one who speaks "peace to your mind" (D&C 6:23). In delivering God's guiding empathy and succor to us, it is he, the Holy Ghost, who will "show unto you all things what ye should do" (2 Nephi 32:5). *When we speak of God understanding and helping us, we speak of the common work of the Holy Ghost in comforting, teaching, and directing us.* True to the Faith puts it this way: "As the soothing voice of a loving parent can quiet a crying child, the whisperings of the Spirit can calm your fears, hush the nagging worries of your life, and comfort you when you grieve."[14] When we sing and pray to God, "Lead me, guide me, walk beside me,"[15] we seem to actually be singing and praying for the Holy Ghost to come, who will whisper "a word behind thee, saying, This is the way, walk ye in it" (Isaiah 30:21) and who "will guide you into all truth" (John 16:13).

The Holy Ghost and Strengthening

Perhaps the best articulation of the strengthening and enabling power of Christ delivered to us through the Holy Ghost is this classic quote from Elder Parley P. Pratt, who so poetically described the myriad of ways the Holy Ghost delivers the strengthening power of Christ: "The gift of the Holy Spirit . . . quickens all the intellectual faculties, increases, enlarges, expands and purifies all the natural passions and affections; and adapts them, by the gift of wisdom, to their lawful use. It inspires, develops, cultivates and matures all the fine-toned sympathies, joys, tastes, kindred feelings and affections of our nature. It inspires virtue, kindness, goodness, tenderness, gentleness and charity. It develops beauty of person, form and features. It tends to health, vigor, animation and social feeling. It develops and invigorates all the faculties of the physical and intellectual man. It strengthens, invigorates, and gives tone to the nerves. In short, it is, as it were, marrow to the bone, joy to the heart, light to the eyes, music to the ears, and life to the whole being."[16]

Who would have thought that the Holy Ghost can perform such strengthening wonders in our life—increasing the capacity of our spiritual, intellectual, and physical person—apparently even making us better looking! The scriptures are emphatic on the connection between the strengthening power of Christ and the Holy Ghost. Note the relationship between strength from God beyond our natural capacity being given (or taken) and the Holy Spirit in each of the following verses:

- "But this is not all; they had given themselves to much prayer, and fasting; therefore they had the *spirit of prophecy, and the spirit of revelation,* and when they taught, they taught with *power* and authority of God" (Alma 17:3; emphasis added).
- "Nevertheless the strength of the Lord was not with us; yea, we were left to ourselves, that *the Spirit of the Lord did not abide in us;* therefore *we had become weak* like unto our brethren" (Mormon 2:26; emphasis added).
- "And it came to pass that Ammon, being filled with the Spirit of God, therefore he perceived the thoughts of the king" (Alma 18:16).
- "And behold, the *Holy Spirit of God* did come down from heaven, and did enter into their hearts, and they were filled as if with fire, and *they could speak forth marvelous words*" (Helaman 5:45; emphasis added).
- "And Alma went forth, and also Amulek, among the people, to declare the words of God unto them;

and they were filled with the Holy Ghost. And they had power given unto them, insomuch that they could not be confined in dungeons; neither was it possible that any man could slay them. . . . Now, this was done that the Lord might show forth his power in them" (Alma 8:30–31; emphasis added).

Even one of the greatest miracles in all of scriptural history, Moses parting the Red Sea, was a result of the guiding power of the Holy Ghost (see D&C 8:2–3). I would not doubt if in some way all miracles—whether it be parting the Red Sea or walking on water or translating the Book of Mormon—were and are a result of the Holy Ghost infusing God's children with divine power beyond their natural capacity (see Alma 26:12). Even the holy miracle of Jesus's divine birth was "by the power of the Holy Ghost" (Alma 7:10).

This extra-human capacity from the Spirit of God doesn't apply only to miracles. Even our ordinary everyday skills and abilities are enhanced by the Spirit of God delivering the strengthening power of Christ. The First Presidency has said: "We promise that as you keep [the Lord's] standards, you will be blessed with the companionship of the Holy Ghost."[17] This promise of inspiration and strength from the Holy Ghost applies, as Elder Pratt's earlier quote suggests, to all aspects of our lives: in work, school, family, church, athletics, the arts, and the like. When we "perform any thing unto the Lord" (2 Nephi 32:9), the Spirit can strengthen us. Perhaps most importantly, the Holy Ghost is the armor bearer of the shield of faith to strengthen us against temptation and evil. *Gospel*

Fundamentals teaches that "the Holy Ghost also gives us strength to obey the commandments of our Father in Heaven and Jesus."[18] The First Presidency summarized it this way: "The Holy Ghost will give you strength to make correct choices."[19] As the messenger of the Almighty, the Holy Ghost is indeed the spirit of strength.

The Holy Ghost and Transforming

I have been equal parts excited, fascinated, terrified, nauseated, scared, and inspired at the birth of each of our children—and I was only a spectator. The spirituality of the birth of a newborn, however, has never ceased to amaze me. Here they are, these slippery, swollen, purple-pinkish, flailing and wailing creatures being poked and prodded and measured and cleaned and wrapped within their first hour of mortality, and yet despite it all there is a reverence there. In fact, at the birth of our fifth child, the power of the Spirit in the room was so overwhelming as to be almost tangible. *Sacred* would be an apt word to describe it. Yes, in a birth there is blood. Yes, there are lots of fluids. But oh! above all, there is a new spirit.

Using our first birth as an analogy, the Lord has told all of us that in our lifetime we must be "born again" (John 3:7). And, once again, yes, there is to be blood, there is to be water, and of necessity there has to be the Spirit. The Lord taught Adam, "Inasmuch as ye were born into the world by water, and blood, and the spirit, which I have made, and so became of dust a living soul, even so ye must be born again into the kingdom of heaven, of water, and of the Spirit, and be cleansed by blood, even the blood of mine Only Begotten" (Moses 6:59). *The spiritual rebirth we all must have is carried to term by the power of the Holy Ghost.* Just as a mother's womb provides the natural environment to enable our mortal birth, when our lives are encircled by the power of the Holy Ghost, his steady influence provides the spiritual environment which brings about a change to our very nature through his heavenly power. Note the relationship between the transforming power of Christ and the Holy Ghost in this statement by King Benjamin's people: "And they all cried with one voice, saying: Yea, we believe all the words which thou hast spoken unto us; and also, we know of their surety and truth, *because of the Spirit of the Lord Omnipotent, which has wrought a mighty change in us, or in our hearts,* that we have no more disposition to do evil, but to do good continually" (Mosiah 5:2; emphasis added). Paul called our converting change the "renewing of the Holy Ghost" (Titus 3:5).

Just as a mother's womb provides the natural environment to enable our mortal birth, when our lives are encircled by the power of the Holy Ghost, his steady influence provides the spiritual environment which brings about a change to our very nature through his heavenly power.

Alma the Younger—an expert on being born again—said of his own conversion that he had been "redeemed of the Lord; behold, *I am born of the Spirit*" (Mosiah 27:24; emphasis added). On another occasion Alma explained the transformation that took place in faithful high priests: "Now they, *after being sanctified by the Holy Ghost,* having their garments made white, being pure and spotless before God, could not look upon sin save it were with abhorrence"

(Alma 13:12; emphasis added). Connecting the gift of tasting charity, note how Alma explained that he wished to "bring [others] to taste of the exceeding joy of which I did taste; that they might also be born of God, and be filled with the Holy Ghost" (Alma 36:24). Tasting charity, being born again, and being filled with the Holy Ghost are interrelated. Elder M. Russell Ballard explained: "True conversion comes through the power of the Spirit. When the Spirit touches the heart, hearts are changed."[20] Daily, righteous, repeated actions invite the Holy Ghost into our life, and its steady and repeated influence on our mind, heart, and character transform us to become "partakers of the divine nature" (2 Peter 1:4).

The Agent of the Atonement

Summarizing President Henry B. Eyring's statement from earlier in the chapter in my own words, if the Holy Ghost's influence is present in your life, then the gifts, powers, and promises of the Atonement of Jesus Christ are also in operation in your life. *The members of the Godhead are inseparably linked. If you receive the one, you will receive the other (see John 13:20; D&C 84:37).* Nephi suggested this interdependent relationship in 1 Nephi 10. To help make the connection between receiving Christ and receiving the Holy Ghost more apparent, I've substituted the name of Christ for pronouns in brackets [like this] for clarity:

"And it came to pass after I, Nephi, having heard all the words of my father, concerning the things which he saw in a vision, and also the things which he spake *by the power of the Holy Ghost, which power he received by faith on the Son of God*—and the Son of God was the Messiah who should come—I, Nephi, was desirous also that I might see, and hear, and know of these things, *by the power of the Holy Ghost, which is the gift of God unto all those who diligently seek [Christ]*, as well in times of old as in the time that [Christ] should manifest himself unto the children of men. . . . *For he that diligently seeketh [Christ] shall find [Christ]; and the mysteries of God shall be unfolded unto them, by the power of the Holy Ghost*" (1 Nephi 10:17, 19; emphasis added).

The gift of the Holy Ghost unfolds the mysteries and powers of Christ to all who seek the Savior. It was revealed to Joseph Smith that in our mortal, day-to-day lives the "power[s] of godliness" can be extended to mankind in the flesh (see D&C 84:20). These powers of godliness are the atoning powers of Christ,[21] which "'power of godliness' comes in the person and by the influence of the Holy Ghost," as Elder D. Todd Christofferson has said.[22]

So, who wants to be cleansed from the stain of sin? Who wants to be healed from sickness, sin, and sorrow? Who wants hope and assurance in the eternal promises of God? Who wants to be understood and guided? Who wants to be strengthened and helped by Jesus's grace? Who wants to be changed and transformed into a holier person—spiritually born again? In summary: Who wants to receive the everyday powers of Christ? If we do, then we must receive the messenger of mercy, the deliverer of divinity, the representative of the Redeemer, the agent of the Atonement, the giver of grace: the Holy Ghost.

ACKNOWLEDGMENTS

This book is the result of many hands, each contributing in their own unique and valuable way. I extend my gratitude in particular to the following: At Deseret Book, Lisa Roper for believing in me and this manuscript and for her suggestions to improve the initial drafts; Derk Koldewyn for the excellent editorial work in making the manuscript more readable; Rachael Ward for the typesetting; and Shauna Gibby for the layout design. At BYU, my colleagues John Hilton III, Brad Wilcox, and Greg Wilkinson for reading various chapters and giving feedback that strengthened the book and Dr. Robert Millet for a careful review of the entire manuscript wherein he provided invaluable doctrinal and writing improvements. My research assistants, Nicole Wechsler and Jordan Hadley, for their reviews and source checking. My friends Emily Thevenin and Brandon Gunnell for their reading of and thoughts on the healing power chapter. Last, to my wife, Cindy, for her unfailing support, insights, critiques, and encouragement through every draft and aspect of this project. My love and gratitude to each of you.

NOTES

INTRODUCTION
The Ever-Present Powers of Christ

1. Annie S. Hawkes, "I Need Thee Every Hour," *Hymns of The Church of Jesus Christ of Latter-day Saints* (Salt Lake City: The Church of Jesus Christ of Latter-day Saints, 1985), no. 98.
2. Boyd K. Packer, "'The Touch of the Master's Hand,'" *Ensign*, May 2001, 22.

CHAPTER 1
The Cleansing Power of Christ

Epigraph. Cited in *Forty Thousand Sublime and Beautiful Thoughts: Gathered from the Roses, Clover Blossoms, Geraniums, Violets, Morning Glories, and Pansies of Literature*, compiled by Charles Noel Douglas (New York: The Christian Herald Bible House, 1915), 759.
1. John MacArthur, *The Gospel According to Jesus* (Grand Rapids, MI: Zondervan, 2008), 79.
2. Jeffrey R. Holland, "The Laborers in the Vineyard," *Ensign*, May 2012, 33.
3. Craig A. Cardon, "The Savior Wants to Forgive," *Ensign*, May 2013, 16.
4. Karen Lynn Davidson, David J. Whitaker, Mark Ashurst-McGee, and Richard L. Jensen, eds., *The Joseph Smith Papers: Histories, Volume 1: 1832–1844* (Salt Lake City: Church Historian's Press, 2012), 13; formatting standardized.
5. Tad R. Callister, "How Do I Know When I'm Forgiven?"; available at https://www.lds.org/youth/article/how-do-i-know-when-i-am-forgiven?lang=eng; accessed 2 November 2015.
6. See D. Todd Christofferson, "The Power of Covenants," *Ensign*, May 2009, 20.

7. *Preach My Gospel* (Salt Lake City: The Church of Jesus Christ of Latter-day Saints, 2004), 62.

8. Boyd K. Packer, *Mine Errand from the Lord* (Salt Lake City: Deseret Book, 2008), 196.

9. Dallin H. Oaks, "The Aaronic Priesthood and the Sacrament," *Ensign*, November 1998, 37.

10. Jörg Klebingat, "Approaching the Throne of God with Confidence," *Ensign*, November 2014, 37.

CHAPTER 2

The Healing Power of Christ

Epigraph. Dallin H. Oaks, "He Heals the Heavy Laden," *Ensign*, November 2006, 8.

1. The top four denominations to report having experienced or witnessed a divine healing, in order, were: 1. LDS (69 percent); 2. Other Christian (60 percent); 3. Historically black churches (55 percent); 4. Evangelical churches (51 percent). See "U.S. Religious Landscape Survey: Religious Affiliation: Diverse and Dynamic," *The Pew Forum on Religion and Public Life*, February 2008, 188; and also "U.S. Religious Landscape Survey: Religious Beliefs and Practices: Diverse and Politically Relevant," *The Pew Forum on Religion and Public Life*, June 2008, 54.

2. As cited in Oaks, "Healing the Sick," *Ensign*, May 2010, 50.

3. Russell M. Nelson, "Jesus Christ—The Master Healer," *Ensign*, November 2005, 87.

4. Wendy Ulrich, *The Temple Experience: Our Journey Toward Holiness* (Springville, UT: Cedar Fort, 2012), 8–9.

5. Michele Reyes, "Whole Enough," *Ensign*, January 2013, 14.

6. Reyes, "Whole Enough," 14.

7. Reyes, "Whole Enough," 14–15.

8. Emily Thevenin, "Am I of Worth?" *Ensign*, July 2009, 8.

9. "President Kimball Speaks Out on Administration to the Sick," *New Era*, October 1981, 47.

10. "Faith," in *True to the Faith* (Salt Lake City: The Church of Jesus Christ of Latter-day Saints, 2004), 54.

11. There are a few scriptural cases, however, when iniquity did cause infirmity, such as Zeezrom's fever, the Philistines' tumors, and Gehazi's leprosy (see Alma 15:1–3; 1 Samuel 5:1–9; and 2 Kings 5:20–27, respectively).

12. Richard G. Scott, "To Heal the Shattering Consequences of Abuse," *Ensign*, May 2008, 43.

13. Mary A. Pepper Kidder, "Did You Think to Pray?" *Hymns*, no. 140.

14. Shayne M. Bowen, "'Because I Live, Ye Shall Live Also,'" *Ensign*, November 2012, 17.

15. See Nelson, "Why This Holy Land?" *Ensign*, December 1989, 17–18.

16. See Oaks, "Healing the Sick," 50.

17. David A. Bednar, "We Believe in Being Chaste," *Ensign*, May 2013, 44.

18. *For the Strength of Youth* (Salt Lake City: The Church of Jesus Christ of Latter-day Saints, 2012), 37.

19. Bednar, "We Believe in Being Chaste," 44.

20. See Neal A. Maxwell, "'Lest Ye Be Wearied and Faint in Your Minds,'" *Ensign*, May 1991, 90.

21. Thanks to Emily Thevenin for her ideas about being still and its relationship to healing. This paragraph is a result of my dialogue with her.

CHAPTER 3
The Restoring Power of Christ

Epigraph. Phillip Yancey, *The Jesus I Never Knew* (Grand Rapids, MI: Zondervan, 2002), 267.

1. Linda Reeves, "Claim the Blessings of Your Covenants," *Ensign*, November 2013, 119.

2. "Atonement of Jesus Christ," in *True to the Faith* (Salt Lake City: The Church of Jesus Christ of Latter-day Saints, 2004), 14.

3. See Alister E. McGrath, *Christian Literature: An Anthology* (Malden, MA: Wiley-Blackwell, 2001), 357.

4. James E. Talmage, "The Eternity of Sex," *Young Woman's Journal*, Volume 25 (October 1914): 603.

5. Richard G. Scott, "Jesus Christ, Our Redeemer," *Ensign*, May 1997, 53.

6. *Teachings of the Prophet Joseph Smith*, sel. Joseph Fielding Smith (Salt Lake City: Deseret Book, 1976), 296.

7. Boyd K. Packer, "The Brilliant Morning of Forgiveness," *Ensign*, November 1995, 19–20.

8. Elizabeth Smart with Chris Stewart, *My Story* (New York: St. Martin's Press, 2013), 285–86; paragraphing altered.

9. Smart, *My Story*, 304–5; emphasis added, paragraphing altered.

10. Name withheld, "Forgiveness and Making Up for Losses," *Ensign*, August 2012, 61; the name *Kaylee* in the *Ensign* story is a pseudonym.

11. William Nicholson, Alain Boublil, Claude-Michel Schönberg, and Herbert Kretzmer (screenwriters); Tom Hooper (director), *Les Misérables* (Los Angeles: Universal, 2012).

12. *Handbook 2: Administering the Church*, "Unmarried Members of the Church" (Salt Lake City: The Church of Jesus Christ of Latter-day Saints, 2010), 1.3.3.

CHAPTER 4
The Identifying Power of Christ

1. See John MacArthur, *The MacArthur New Testament Commentary, John 1–11* (Chicago: Moody Publishers, 2006), 41.

2. Merriam-Webster's Eleventh Collegiate Dictionary (Springfield, MA: Merriam-Webster, 2003), s.v. "condescend."
3. See James E. Talmage, *Jesus the Christ* (Salt Lake City: Deseret Book, 1915), 105.
4. See Dallin H. Oaks, "Sins and Mistakes," *Ensign*, October 1996, 62–67.
5. Edward Shillito, "Jesus of the Scars"; as cited in D. A. Carson, *How Long, O Lord? Reflections on Suffering and Evil* (Grand Rapids, MI: Baker Books, 2006), 170.
6. For an excellent read on the nature of Jesus's atoning suffering, I would recommend *The Infinite Atonement* (Salt Lake City: Deseret Book, 2002) by Tad R. Callister, particularly chapter 14, "Infinite in Suffering."
7. Neal A. Maxwell, "'Willing to Submit,'" *Ensign*, May 1985, 72–73.
8. Merrill J. Bateman, "The Power to Heal from Within," *Ensign*, May 1995, 14.
9. See Bateman, "The Power to Heal From Within," 14. See also Bateman, "One by One," *BYU Magazine*, Spring 1998, 5.
10. David A. Bednar, "Bear Up Their Burdens with Ease," *Ensign*, May 2014, 90.
11. Edward Hopper, "Jesus, Savior, Pilot Me," *Hymns*, no. 104.
12. Maxwell, "'Yet Thou Art There,'" *Ensign*, November 1987, 32.
13. Jeffrey R. Holland, "Lessons from Liberty Jail," Brigham Young University fireside, 7 September 2008; available at https://speeches.byu.edu/talks/jeffrey-r-holland_lessons-liberty-jail/; accessed 2 November 2015.
14. Maxwell, *Even As I Am* (Salt Lake City: Deseret Book, 1982), 116–17.

CHAPTER 5

The Strengthening Power of Christ

1. "Last Testimony of Sister Emma," *Saints' Herald*, vol. 26, no. 19 (October 1, 1879): 290.
2. Grace is the "free and unmerited favor of God" (Google), also "unmerited divine assistance" (*Merriam-Webster's Eleventh Collegiate Dictionary*) or, closer to our Bible Dictionary definition: "Divine favor bestowed freely on people . . . An excellence or power granted by God" (thefreedictionary.com).
3. Bible Dictionary, s.v. "Grace," 697.
4. See David A. Bednar, "Bear Up Their Burdens with Ease," *Ensign*, May 2014, 87–90; "Clean Hands and a Pure Heart," *Ensign*, November 2007, 80–83; and "'In the Strength of the Lord,'" Brigham Young University devotional address, 23 October 2001 (available at https://speeches.byu.edu/talks/david-a-bednar_strength-lord/), for a few excellent examples.
5. Bednar, "'In the Strength of the Lord,'" *Ensign*, November 2004, 76.
6. Susan Evans McCloud, "Lord, I Would Follow Thee," *Hymns*, no. 220.
7. See Jay A. Parry, Jack M. Lyon, and Linda R. Gundry, eds., *Best-Loved Stories of the LDS People, Vol. 2* (Salt Lake City: Deseret Book, 2001), 125–27.
8. M. Russell Ballard, "Be Strong in the Lord," *Ensign*, July 2004, 11–12.
9. Evan Stephens, "In Remembrance of Thy Suffering," *Hymns*, no. 183.

10. See Boyd K. Packer, "How to Survive in Enemy Territory," *New Era*, April 2012, 3.

11. Bible Dictionary, s.v. "Grace," 697.

12. Neal A. Maxwell, "It's Service, Not Status, That Counts," *Ensign*, July 1975, 7.

13. See James E. Faust, "Five Loaves and Two Fishes," *Ensign*, May 1994, 5.

14. John Wilmot, retrieved from http://thinkexist.com/quotation/before_i_got _married_i_had_six_theories_about/12508.html.

15. "Go Forward with Faith," in *For the Strength of Youth* (Salt Lake City: The Church of Jesus Christ of Latter-day Saints, 2011), 43.

16. Bill Wilson, "The Twelve Step of Alcoholics Anonymous," A. A. World Services, Inc. (revised 6/14); available at http://www.aa.org/pages/en_US/what-is-aa; accessed 3 November 2015.

17. See LDS Family Services, *Addiction Recovery Program: A Guide to Addiction Recovery and Healing* (Salt Lake City: The Church of Jesus Christ of Latter-day Saints, 2005), iv.

18. *Addiction Recovery Program*, 36; emphasis added.

19. Adam S. Miller, *Rube Goldberg Machines: Essays in Mormon Theology* (Draper, UT: Greg Kofford Books, 2012), 100.

20. Miller, *Rube Goldberg Machines*, 104.

CHAPTER 6

The Transforming Power of Christ

Epigraph. Joseph B. Wirthlin, "The Great Commandment," *Ensign*, November 2007, 30.

1. As cited by David A. Bednar in "'In the Strength of the Lord,'" BYU devotional address, 23 October 2001; available at https://speeches.byu.edu/talks/david-a-bednar _strength-lord/; accessed 3 November 2015.

2. *Merriam-Webster's Eleventh Collegiate Dictionary*, s.v. "Redeem."

3. *Joseph Smith* [manual], in Teachings of the Presidents of the Church series (Salt Lake City: The Church of Jesus Christ of Latter-day Saints, 2007), 210.

4. "Plan of Salvation," in *True to the Faith* (Salt Lake City: The Church of Jesus Christ of Latter-day Saints, 2004), 115.

5. Lorenzo Snow, *The Teachings of Lorenzo Snow*, Clyde J. Williams, ed. (Salt Lake City: Bookcraft, 1984), 1.

6. See Bruce R. McConkie, *Mormon Doctrine*, 2d ed. (Salt Lake City: Bookcraft, 1966), 237.

7. "Conversion," in *True to the Faith*, 41.

8. Stephen Buttry, "Des Moines Register: Candidates focus on Christian beliefs"; available at http://archives.cnn.com/1999/ALLPOLITICS/stories/12/15 /religion.register/; accessed 3 November 2015.

9. See "Conversion," in *True to the Faith*, 41–42.

10. D. Todd Christofferson, "Born Again," *Ensign*, May 2008, 78.

11. See Bednar, "Ye Must Be Born Again," *Ensign*, May 2007, 19–22.

12. Joseph Alleine, *An Alarm to the Unconverted*, 2002 reprint edition, Jay P. Green, ed. (Lafayette, IN: Sovereign Grace Publishers, 2002), 9.

13. See *The Autobiography of Benjamin Franklin* (Boston: Houghton, Mifflin and Company, 1888), 102–14.

14. Some Bible translations quote Jesus's stinging rebuke about Nicodemus's understanding (John 3:10) as, "'You are Israel's teacher,' said Jesus, 'and do you not understand these things?'" (New International Version) or "'Are you the teacher of Israel and yet you do not understand these things?'" (English Standard Version), implying that Nicodemus may have been one of the preeminent teachers in all of Israel at this time.

15. *Millennial Star,* vol. 56, no. 17 (23 April 1894): 260.

16. Bible Dictionary, s.v. "Charity," 632.

17. H. G. Liddell and Robert Scott, *An Intermediate Greek-English Lexicon: Founded Upon the Seventh Edition of Liddell and Scott's Greek-English Lexicon* (Oxford: Benediction Classics, 2010), 4.

18. Dieter F. Uchtdorf, "The Merciful Obtain Mercy," *Ensign*, May 2012, 75; paragraphing altered.

19. M. Russell Ballard, "O That Cunning Plan of the Evil One," *Ensign*, November 2010, 110.

20. Brigham Young University communications professor Mark Callister used this metaphor in his BYU devotional address titled "Lost and Found," 7 October 2014.

21. Gordon B. Hinckley, "Let Us Live the Gospel More Fully," *Ensign*, November 2003, 102.

22. John A. Widtsoe, in Conference Report, April 1952, 34.

23. Russell M. Nelson, "Thanks Be to God," *Ensign*, May 2012, 79.

24. Dallin H. Oaks, "The Challenge to Become," *Ensign*, November 2000, 32–34.

25. *Joseph Smith* [manual], 330–31.

CONCLUSION

The Agent of Christ's Atonement: The Holy Ghost

1. See David A. Bednar, "Teach Them to Understand," Ricks College Campus Education Week devotional, 4 June 1998; available at http://www2.byui.edu /Presentations/Transcripts/EducationWeek/1998_06_04_Bednar.htm; accessed 3 November 2015.

2. Henry B. Eyring, "Gifts of the Spirit for Hard Times," *Ensign*, June 2007, 23.

3. Eyring, "Come unto Christ," Brigham Young University fireside, 29 October 1989; available at https://speeches.byu.edu/talks/henry-b-eyring_come-unto -christ/; accessed 3 November 2015.

4. D. Todd Christofferson, "The Power of Covenants," *Ensign*, May 2009, 22.

5. Nita Dale Milner, "When I Am Baptized," *Children's Songbook of The Church of*

Jesus Christ of Latter-day Saints (Salt Lake City: The Church of Jesus Christ of Latter-day Saints, 1989), 103.

6. Bruce R. McConkie, *A New Witness for the Articles of Faith* (Salt Lake City: Deseret Book, 1985), 290.

7. McConkie, *A New Witness for the Articles of Faith*, 239.

8. Christofferson, "The Divine Gift of Repentance," *Ensign*, November 2011, 40.

9. Eyring, "Come unto Christ."

10. "The Holy Ghost acts as a cleansing agent to purify," Bible Dictionary, s.v. "Holy Ghost," 704.

11. Eyring, "Gifts of the Spirit for Hard Times," *Ensign*, June 2007, 23.

12. See Dallin H. Oaks, "The Aaronic Priesthood and the Sacrament," *Ensign*, November 1998, 37.

13. See Elaine S. Dalton, "A Return to Virtue," *Ensign*, November 2008, 78–80.

14. "The Holy Ghost," in *True to the Faith*, 82.

15. Naomi W. Randall, "I Am a Child of God," *Hymns*, no. 301.

16. Parley P. Pratt, *Key to the Science of Theology*, 9th ed. (Salt Lake City: Deseret Book, 1965), 101.

17. "Message to the Youth from The First Presidency," in *For the Strength of Youth* (Salt Lake City: The Church of Jesus Christ of Latter-day Saints, 2011), ii.

18. "The Holy Ghost," in *Gospel Fundamentals* (Salt Lake City: The Church of Jesus Christ of Latter-day Saints, 2002); available at https://www.lds.org/manual/gospel-fundamentals/chapter-7-the-holy-ghost?lang=eng; accessed 3 November 2015.

19. "Entertainment and the Media," in *For the Strength of Youth*, 13.

20. M. Russell Ballard, "Now Is the Time," *Ensign*, November 2000, 75.

21. David A. Bednar taught, "And what is the power of godliness? The blessings of the Atonement" ("A Discussion with Elder David A. Bednar," CES Training Broadcast, 2 August 2011).

22. Christofferson, "The Power of Covenants," 22.

INDEX

Addiction Recovery Program, 107
Agapē, 127
Alcoholics Anonymous, 107
Alleine, Joseph, 123
Alma the Younger, 102, 151–52
Angels, 111
Art, restoration of, 103
Atonement: ever-present power of, 1–4;
    restoration through, 51–54, 55, 66;
    and identifying power of Jesus Christ,
    79–82; Holy Ghost and, 138–39,
    152–53

Ballard, M. Russell, 103, 129, 152
Baptism and baptismal covenant, 16, 140,
    141
Bateman, Merrill J., 80
Bednar, David A., 41, 42, 81–82, 96–97
Beecher, Henry Ward, 7
Birth, 150. *See also* Rebirth
Bishops, 41
Book of Mormon: healings in, 29–30, 45;
    examples of divine strength in, 96, 97,
    100–101

Bowen, Shane, 39–40
Bush, George W., 120

Caitlin, 101–2
Callings, 104–5
Callister, Tad R., 14
Cana, miracle at, 115–17
Cannon, George Q., 126
Challenges, being strengthened through,
    99–102
Change. *See* Transforming power of
    Christ
Change of heart, 39–40, 119–21, 125,
    129–30, 133, 152. *See also* Conversion;
    Rebirth; Transforming power of
    Christ
Charity, 101–2, 126–30, 134–35
Christ, as title, 132
Christlike attributes, 55–59, 64
Christofferson, D. Todd, 122, 139, 140,
    153
Church activity, receiving healing power
    through, 40–41
Cleansing power of Christ: need for, 5,
    7–10; sins freely forgiven through,

10–11; sins frequently forgiven through, 11–13; sins fully forgiven through, 13–15; attaining, 15–17; retaining, 18–21; rejoicing in, 22–23; further study suggestions regarding, 23–25; and transforming power of Christ, 131, 132; Holy Ghost and, 140–42. *See also* Forgiveness; Repentance

Compassion, 10, 46, 88

Condescension of Jesus Christ, 73–74, 89

Conversion, 119–26, 128–29, 134, 151–52. *See also* Change of heart; Rebirth; Transforming power of Christ

Counsel, seeking, 84–86

Covenant relationship, 16–17

Creative power, healing power and, 45

Cure, versus healing, 32–33

Dedication, 21

Deification, 118, 134

Direction, seeking, 84–86

Easter, 49

Emotions, of Jesus Christ, 89

Empathy, 79, 81, 84, 85, 87–88. *See also* Identifying power of Christ

Enos, 35

Eyring, Henry B., 138–39, 142

Ezekiel, 125–26

Faith: healing and, 31, 37–43; in strengthening power of Christ, 109–10

Fall of Adam and Eve, 51, 52–53, 54, 62, 65–66

Feelings, of Jesus Christ, 89

First Presidency, 106, 118, 149, 150

Forgiveness: possibility of, 5, 9–10; given freely, 10–11, 24; given frequently, 11–13, 24; given fully, 13–15, 24; and restoring power of Jesus Christ,

55–58, 60–61. *See also* Cleansing power of Christ; Repentance

Future restoration, 64–65, 67

Gethsemane, 7, 80–81, 83, 111

God: mercy of, 10; timing of, 42, 62; trusting in, 108; becoming like, 118, 134; love of, 127–30, 134–35

Godliness, powers of, 153

Good works, strength to do, 104–6

Grace, 96–97

Growing season, 62–64

Halloween, 31

Hand washing, 115–16

Harvest, law of, 59–60

Hawkes, Annie S., 1

Healing power of Christ: attaining, 27; in scriptures, 29–30; in modern day, 30; and remaining infirmity, 30–32, 45; and healing as wholeness, 32–35; and spiritual healing, 36–37; faith and, 37–43; and healing of nations, 43–44; further study suggestions regarding, 44–46; and transforming power of Christ, 131; Holy Ghost and, 142–44

Heart, change of, 39–40, 119–21, 125, 129–30, 133, 152

Hezekiah, 39

Hinckley, Gordon B., 130–31

Holland, Jeffrey R., 10, 85

Holy Ghost: gift of, 125; and transforming power of Christ, 126, 150–52; role of, 137–39; and cleansing power of Christ, 140–42; and healing power of Christ, 142–44; and restoring power of Christ, 144–46; and identifying power of Christ, 146–47; and strengthening power of Christ, 147–50; as agent of Atonement, 152–53

Hope, 145

Hugo, Victor, 113
Humanity of Jesus Christ, 74–75, 78, 88–89
Humility, 39, 107

Identifying power of Christ, 69, 71–73; and condescension of Jesus Christ, 73–74; and humanity of Jesus Christ, 74–75; and Jesus's temptations and mistakes, 75–79; and suffering of Jesus Christ, 79–82; and understanding and support of Jesus Christ, 82–84, 86–87; and seeking direction in daily lives, 84–86; further study suggestions regarding, 87–89; and transforming power of Christ, 131; Holy Ghost and, 146–47
Inequity, 47, 54–55, 64–65
Infinity, 17

"Jesus of the Scars" (Shillito), 78–79
Joseph, 63

Karma, 59–60
Kimball, Spencer W., 37–38
Klebingat, Jörg, 25
Knowledge, of Jesus Christ, 76–78, 88–89

Law of the harvest, 59–60
Lepers, 35
Les Misérables (Hugo), 64, 113
"Let the Holy Spirit Guide," 143
Loneliness, 89
Losses, restoration of, 54–59, 66–67
Love, 127–30, 134–35

MacArthur, John, 8
Marriage, 15–16, 18–19, 24–25
Maxwell, Neal A., 42, 80, 83, 85, 105
McConkie, Bruce R., 140
McKay, David O., 117

Melchizedek priesthood, 45
Mercy, 10, 61, 62. See also Restoring power of Christ
Miller, Adam, 107–8
Millet, Robert L., 81
Ministering angels, 111
Miracle at Cana, 115–17
Mistakes of Jesus Christ, 75–79
Monson, Thomas S., 49
Mortality: suffering as part of, 31–32; unfairness in, 47, 54–55, 64–65; Jesus's experience in, 72–73, 89–90; and humanity of Jesus Christ, 74–75; Jesus's temptations and mistakes in, 75–79; purpose of, 117–18
Moses, 45
Mother, accesses strengthening power of Christ, 98–99

Nations, healing of, 43–44
Natural man, 121, 126
Nelson, Russell M., 32, 133
Nephi, 93–95, 109, 110, 152–53
New Testament, examples of divine strength in, 96, 97
Nicodemus, 124–25, 160n14

Oaks, Dallin H., 21, 29, 46, 134
Obedience: receiving healing power through, 38–39; of Jesus Christ, 77–78
Old Testament: healings in, 29–30, 44; examples of divine strength in, 95, 100

Packer, Boyd K., 1, 20–21, 55
Paintings, restoration of, 103
Parenting, 105–6
Patience: in healing, 41–42; in restoration, 66
Paul, 112
Perfection, 21

Peter, 108

Pharisee, 7–8

Plan of salvation, 117

Powers of godliness, 153

Pratt, Parley P., 147

Prayer: and retaining cleansing power of Christ, 19–20; receiving healing power through, 39–40; for counsel and direction, 85–86

Priesthood, receiving healing power through, 40, 45, 46

Provo City Center Temple, 49–50

Publican, 7–8

Rebirth, 119–26, 134, 150–51. *See also* Change of heart; Conversion; Transforming power of Christ

Redemption, 50–51, 117

Reeves, Linda, 51

Repentance: possibility of, 5, 9–10; need for, 8–9; and retaining cleansing power of Christ, 18–21; real, 25; and growing season, 62; baptism and, 140. *See also* Cleansing power of Christ; Forgiveness

Restoring power of Christ: attaining, 47; Provo City Center Temple as example of, 49–50; redemption through, 50–51; Atonement and, 51–54; mortal wrongs made right through, 54–55, 64–65; and becoming more Christlike, 55–59; sowing and growing seasons and, 59–64; further study suggestions regarding, 65–67; and transforming power of Christ, 131; Holy Ghost and, 144–46

Resurrection, 52–54, 55, 143

Reyes, Michele, 33–34

Righteous: need cleansing power of Christ, 7–9; self-perception as, 23–24

Rocks, identifying, 71

Sacrament, 20–21

Samaritan lepers, 35

Scott, Richard G., 39, 54

Scriptures: examples of divine strength in, 95–96, 100–101, 110, 148–49; examples of conversion in, 121–22; and spiritual healing, 144

Shillito, Edward, 78–79

Ship, Nephi commanded to build, 93–94, 109

Sin(s): as freely forgiven, 10–11, 24; as frequently forgiven, 11–13, 24; as fully forgiven, 13–15, 24; Atonement and, 52; versus error, 76–77; strength to overcome, 102–4, 111; baptism and, 140, 141. *See also* Cleansing power of Christ; Forgiveness; Repentance

Smart, Elizabeth, 56–57

Smith, Joseph: forgiveness of, 12; on restoration in resurrection, 55; on plan of salvation, 118; on love of God, 135

Snow, Lorenzo, 118

Sowing season, 59–61

Spiritual healing, 36–37, 41–43, 144

Spiritually flawed people: need cleansing power of Christ, 9–10; self-perception as, 23–24

Stillness, receiving healing power through, 42–43

Strengthening power of Christ: help through, 91, 93–94; need for, 91; Nephi and, 94–95; scriptural examples of, 95–96, 110; accessibility and recipients of, 96–99; and meeting trials and challenges, 99–102; resisting temptation and overcoming sin through, 102–4, 111; performing good works through, 104–6; through weakness, 106–9, 111–12; faith in, 109–10; further study suggestions regarding, 110–12; and transforming power of Christ, 131; Holy Ghost and, 147–50

Strengths, shared in marriage, 15–16

Suffering: as part of mortality, 31–32; and restoring power of Jesus Christ, 50–51; and identifying power of Jesus Christ, 79–82; empathy versus sympathy for, 87–88

Sweat, Calvin, 74

Sweat, Cindy, 15–16

Sweat, Eli, 81

Sympathy, versus empathy, 87–88

Talmage, James E., 53

Temple, receiving healing power through, 41. *See also* Provo City Center Temple

Temptation(s): of Jesus Christ, 75–79; strength to resist, 102–4, 111

Timing, of God, 42, 62

Transforming power of Christ: change possible through, 113; and wedding feast at Cana, 115–17; and plan of salvation, 117–18; rebirth through, 119–26; charity and, 126–30; power of, 130–31; and other powers of Christ, 131–33; further study suggestions regarding, 134–35; Holy

Ghost and, 150–52. *See also* Change of heart; Conversion; Rebirth

Tree bark, stripped, 77

Tree of Life, 43–44

Trials, being strengthened through, 99–102

Trust in God, 108

Tyndale, William, 51–52

Uchtdorf, Dieter F., 129

Ulrich, Wendy, 32–33

Unfairness, 47, 54–55, 64–65, 144–46

Water, turned to wine, 115–17

Weakness, receiving strength through, 106–9, 111–12

Wedding feast at Cana, 115–17

Wholeness, healing as, 32–35

Widtsoe, John A., 131

Will of God, 31

Wine, water turned to, 115–17

Wirthlin, Joseph B., 115

Worship: receiving healing power through, 40–41; how versus what, 88; through emulation, 118

Yancey, Phillip, 49